MEG CANNON
& friends

HOPE
rising
365

Thoughts & reflections
for the whole year

spck

CONTRIBUTORS

Meg Cannon is a spoken-word artist, presenter and film-maker from Essex. She is passionate about creating films and sharing stories that communicate hope. Meg works with schools and charities including Girls' Brigade, Christian Aid and Youthscape to inspire and encourage young people.

Ali Martin is part of the leadership teams for Soul Survivor Watford and Soul Survivor Ministries. She has a particular passion for equipping people to communicate God's word in fresh and engaging ways, and to see the Church moving in the power of the Holy Spirit.

Jessie Faerber is a coach for Resurgo, where she assists 16- to 25-year-olds from disadvantaged backgrounds to find employment. She is the author of *More than Just Pretty* (SPCK, 2018) and the founder of Belle, an organization that works with girls to realize their true value, beauty and purpose.

Naomi Aidoo has a background in secondary school teaching and can be found fulfilling her mission to equip people to live their lives to the full. She is a business coach for faith-focused female leaders and entrepreneurs, and a trustee for Church Mission Society.

Rachael Newham (@RachaelNewham90) is the founder of the Christian mental health charity ThinkTwice and the author of *Learning to Breathe* (SPCK, 2018).

Rachel Gardner is a writer, speaker and director at Youthscape, and President of Girls' Brigade England and Wales. Rachel's contributions are taken from her books *Cherished: Boys, bodies and becoming a girl of gold* (Nottingham: IVP, 2009) and *Beloved* (Nottingham: IVP, 2015).

Ruth Jackson is the editor of *Premier Youth and Children's Work*. She previously worked at CBBC's *Blue Peter* before moving to Ravi Zacharias International Ministries, where she helped set up the youth apologetics strand REBOOT. Ruth is on the leadership team at Holy Trinity, Barnes, and plays bass in The Daisy Chains, an all-female rock and roll band.

For Imogen, Matea, Dasia and Phoebe
May you grow to experience how wide and long and high and deep God's love is for you.

ACKNOWLEDGEMENTS

David: Thank you. You've cheered me on and kept me calm (most of the time — sorry!). You held everything together when I'd disappear to write. I can't say thank you enough.

Mum and Dad: Thanks so much for letting me randomly turn up at 10 p.m. to talk through ideas; it was always so helpful. Your love, encouragement and kindness have always been constant and they've inspired me — thank you!

Sam and Beth: I'm glad I've got you both in my life — thanks for *all* your help over the past 18 months. It's been a juggling act but you've really helped me a lot. Love you both.

Nicci: You're so far away yet you make me feel so cared for — how do you manage that? I love your kind heart and the way you love people. Thanks for regularly checking in to see how I'm doing. Hoping K. grows to love this book; I thought about her a lot as I was writing it.

Catie: Ah, my lovely friend, I'm so pleased you've popped up in my life! I've been extremely grateful for your texts, cards, wise words and hugs — thank you for mentoring me through the highs and lows.

Homegroup: Thank you for praying for me when I've been away writing...
I love you all a lot.

INTRODUCTION

Dear reader,

I'm so pleased that you've got this book in your hands!

Many years ago, I had a dream that I was with a crowd of girls. We were standing together, like an army ready to fight, except we weren't filled with anger, hatred or violence. Instead, we were a family of sisters, ready to fight for kindness, for peace and for love. The crowd was overflowing with excitement — we were about to make a difference, and God was with us.

As you read this book throughout the year, know that we stand together like an army, filled with hope. We can go out and make a difference in the world around us because God is with us.

This book is written by some of the sisters in that army, which stands by you. It's full of stories, reflections, Bible verses and wise words from some really inspiring people. A lot of the contributors are close friends of mine, and their entries are scattered throughout the book. So that you can see who's writing what, I've put their names at the bottom of their pages. If you don't see a name, it'll be me writing to you.

If you come across a page that shares a thought, a verse or a quote, use it as a reflection for the day ahead. You might like to memorize it and carry it with you. God can speak to us through the simplest things.

Whether you read this book from cover to cover or whether you dip in and out of it, I hope it will make you laugh, challenge your thinking and, ultimately, enable you to discover the incredible joy and hope found in God.

I'm cheering you on, I'm with you.

With lots of love,
Meg

COMPLETELY YOU

It's the first day of the year! Woohoo! A whole new year ahead!
How exciting.

At the start of this brand new year, don't be distracted by the loud voices
that say, 'Start a new diet! . . . Get a new style! . . . Have a new haircut! . . .
Be a new you!' You don't need to reinvent yourself and become someone
new. Instead, be determined to be the best *you* that you can be.

So if you really want a resolution, here's one:

*This year try your hardest to be absolutely, entirely, completely you. Nothing
more, nothing less.*

01 JAN

At the break
of the day,
you are there.

THIS IS YOUR LIFE

We often put our lives on hold and wait to be discovered.
We wait for somebody to say, 'It's begun,' 'Now!' or 'This is it.' So much of our teenage years is spent preparing for being a woman, trying to work out who we are and what we'll do with our life. Lots of teenage girls live as if they're backstage all the time, waiting for someone to say,
'Come on, step on to the stage.'

I want to say to you: don't wait for your life to begin — *this* is your life, take up some space and make some noise. You're not here just to decorate the planet, you're here to transform the world. You're here to leave behind a legacy and you will do that just by being yourself and living out your authentic personality.

This is your one wild life.

Rachel

03 JAN

YOU ARE STRONG

One day, I was in the post office and, in front of me in the queue, was a little girl with her mum. This little girl, who was probably about five, began swinging on the metal pole that was dividing the queue. As she did, her mum turned to her and said, 'Grace, please don't swing on that, you're strong and you might pull it over!' In obedience, Grace hopped off the metal platform she was balanced on, and skipped back to her mum with a smile on her face.

I stood in the queue thinking about the words that Grace's mum had used: 'You're strong.' So often as girls (and even grown women!) we're called pretty, gorgeous, cute, sweet but very rarely strong. I so hope that Grace will grow up with a gentle strength and confidence, knowing she has the ability to achieve the dreams she has.

Perhaps you've not had someone in your life like Grace's mum, or maybe you've just forgotten. So let me remind you today . . .

You are strong.

I don't know whether you're feeling capable or useless, weak or strong, excited or worried. What I do know is that you can be completely confident that God is beside you, cheering you on and giving you all the strength and ability you need.

04 JAN

You are complex and unique,
different and wonderful and *full*
of talent to offer the world
(even if you don't believe it).
Remember to be kind
to yourself.

05 JAN

One day
at a
time.

06 JAN

SEEKING GOD

You will seek me and find me when
you seek me with all of your heart.
Jeremiah 29.13

It's a strange idea to think that God can be found. I found it very strange when I read this verse in the Bible when I was about 14. I wrote it on my mirror because it really played on my mind . . . could God really be found? Where is he? So after reading that verse I began looking for him – reading more of the Bible, asking people big life questions, praying, going to church and learning from others about faith.

And since I began my search, I've seen God at work and I recognize more and more that he's with me. I see him in the kindness of people, in the beauty of the sunset; I've felt his peace and I've seen him at work in my relationships. The more I've looked for him, the more I've seen his love running through all areas of my life. I realize that the more I give him my attention, the more I learn about myself.

God *can* be found, and he wants you to find him, so my question today is: are you looking for him? Have you given him any attention? Listen, look, read, pray, ask – and slowly you'll find him and his great life-changing love.

07 JAN

WE NEED YOU

When I was 18, I often worried about what people thought of me. Did they see my crazy curly hair, my broken nose, the teeth that I felt were far too wonky, my pasty white complexion, the spots I had on my chin? What else were people thinking about me? I embarked on a self-improvement programme, wanting to rid myself of anything out of the ordinary.

I wanted to fit in. I ended up in a pretty bad way, and eventually decided to tell three of the amazing women in my life about the state that I was in. They helped me to get back on to my feet and to start to like myself again.

Do you ever feel exhausted by the pressure of trying to fit in? Trying to change to fit the mould that you've been told you need to fit? You are not a project to be worked on; you're not something that needs improving.

It's as though you're a square in one big patchwork quilt: each square is a different colour, a different complicated pattern which has been beautifully designed and made. If all the patchwork squares were the same, the quilt would be plain — and pretty boring, to be honest.

We need you, with all your uniqueness and quirky ways, to be you! And as you learn to live comfortably with yourself you'll give others the permission to do the same. Today, bring your colour, your complex pattern and your uniqueness to the quilt of life, and I promise to keep trying to do the same. Are you with me?

08JAN

Today is a new day,
a fresh start with new opportunities.
There are new people to meet and
new things to learn. Whatever is on
your mind about yesterday or tomorrow,
remember: today is a gift in your hands.

09 JAN

THE NAMES THAT BELONG TO YOU

I know a girl whose dad keeps telling her that she is an accident, a mistake, a waste of space. Another girl I work with is constantly being told by her mum that she won't amount to much, that she needs to be more like her sister, that all she is good at is running away when the going gets tough.

But these statements are lies. They are not what God says about anyone. Even if your parents tell you they didn't want you, even if you are regularly compared to your sister, even if your so-called friends spread untrue rumours about you, the truth about your real identity and value is so amazing. It's amazing because it's true, and it's true because it's what God says.

God says *that he knows and loves you* (1 John 4.9).

God says *that you belong to him as his daughter* (1 John 4.4).

God says *that he knows your potential* (Jeremiah 29.11).

A girl who knows she is 'covered' in labels telling her how much she is loved and how precious she is has no spare space for labels with names like 'disappointment', 'loser' or 'waste of space'. The names that belong to you are: 'lovely', 'cherished', 'unique', 'loved', 'precious', 'beautiful', 'lovable', 'creative'. God covers you with these affirmations because he made you and loves you. This is our true identity.

Rachel

10 JAN

GOD is good, a hiding
place in tough times.
He recognizes and welcomes
anyone looking for help,
No matter how desperate
the trouble.

Nahum 1.7, *The Message*

11 JAN

WHAT ARE YOU LIVING FOR?

One of the biggest and most important questions you can ask yourself is 'What am I here for?' It's a huge question which can leave us feeling slightly (!) overwhelmed. Have you ever thought about it? So many people live for travelling and seeing the world, others live for family, some for getting more 'stuff', some people live for making money, others aim to have the best job, the perfect house — the list goes on and on.

What are you living for?

I truly believe that the only way to discover your purpose is by asking God. The best way to find out how something works would be to ask the inventor; in a similar way I believe the best way to know about ourselves is to ask our Creator.

Spend time with God, asking him, 'Who am I? What do you want me to do with my life?' This is something we need to do regularly, to go back and keep asking, 'What now, Father?' He promises to lead us, just as a shepherd leads and protects his sheep. If you want to know who you are and what you're here for, ask the One who made you and brought you here for this specific time in history. He's created you for a purpose, and a great one at that!

Father,
Thank you for creating me; I am precious to you.
Help me to know the way to be my best and to live a beautiful and full life.

12 JAN

Always remember,
you are loved.

13 JAN.

PRACTISE KINDNESS

An attitude of gratitude
noun
*the quality of being thankful;
readiness to show appreciation
for, and to return, kindness*

Wow! I totally love that definition. I want to be the sort of person who appreciates the people around me and the things I have. An attitude of gratitude takes practice, and it's something we *all* need to work on. So today, as you get up, as you brush your teeth, as you walk, as you meet people, as you eat, as you rest, practise being thankful and be ready to return kindness.

14 JAN

HOW DO YOU DEFINE YOURSELF?

For a long time I defined myself as a *failure*. There were a couple of things I'd tried that hadn't quite gone according to plan, and when they went wrong it was painful. I grew scared to try anything new, to step out in any way in case more failure broke me completely.

The label 'failure' became really hard to wear and the fear became really hard to bear.

But God began to heal me and show me that he had a new identity for me, that making mistakes doesn't have to define me. Isaiah 43.1 says: 'Do not fear, for I have redeemed you; I have summoned you by name; you are mine.' God gave me a new name to live by. Loved, valuable, precious, bold, truth-speaker, an encourager, a secure child of God. And more! How are you defining yourself? Is it 'unlovable', 'lazy', 'not good enough', 'ugly', 'unwanted'? God calls you out of shame and fear. He calls you by your real name. It's time to let go of old labels and take hold of his truth. You are loved and you are his.

Ali

15 JAN

Are you tired?

Worn out?

Burned out on religion?

Come to me. Get away with me and you'll
recover your life. I'll show you how to take a real
rest. Walk with me and work with me — watch how I do
it. Learn the unforced rhythms of grace. I won't lay
anything heavy or ill-fitting on you. Keep company
with me and you'll learn to live freely and lightly.

Matthew 11.28–30, *The Message*

16 JAN

WHAT DO YOU WANT TO ACHIEVE?

There's so much to consider when you think about the word 'achievement', isn't there? It's loaded with so many connotations and not all of them are good. I know there have been times in my life when I've worked so hard to achieve something but it's been for totally wrong reasons. Can you relate? Maybe, like me, you have tried to achieve something like popularity with the 'right' people and have found yourself doing things you wouldn't normally do to get there. Or maybe you've wanted to achieve a certain grade in something and it's meant that you've gone without sleep or taking proper care of yourself in order to achieve your goal.

Now don't get me wrong. I think it's great to aim big and work towards achieving our goals, but I think it's so vital to think about the motivation that's behind our desire to achieve.

Perhaps there's something you want to achieve today. Ask yourself these simple questions so that you can work out where this desire is coming from:

1. Do I have to do anything dishonest in order to achieve my goal?
2. Am I seeking this achievement so that I can impress others, as opposed to desiring it for myself or because I've been called to it?
3. Am I sacrificing looking after myself properly (sleeping, spending time with family and friends, praying, etc.) in order to achieve this goal?

What came up for you? In the Bible, we see people achieve some truly great things. And the Bible actually often speaks about us following the example of those we read about. So, as I said, achievement in and of itself is in no way a bad thing. But it's always important to take some time to think about why you're doing it, what it'll cost and whether or not it's truly worth it. Spend a moment today reflecting on your goals and what you're striving to achieve, and ask God to give you wisdom in your pursuit.

Naomi

17 JAN

CHOOSE KIND WORDS

I met Lucy in 2006 and she quickly became like a sister to me. We made each other laugh uncontrollably, we cried together and shared the most amazing adventures. There was something different about Lucy, and I couldn't put my finger on it — she was just . . . different. Then one day when I was having a bit of a moan about someone, she changed the subject.

It suddenly clicked! I'd never heard Lucy say anything bad about anybody. Ever. Once I'd realized it, I noticed it all the time. If I said something negative about someone, she'd either stay quiet, change the subject or say something like 'Maybe they were having a bad day?'

Lucy's kindness towards others shone a big spotlight on the way I spoke about people. I hadn't realized how often I'd moan or say things that were unkind. So one Monday I decided to spend the whole week saying only kind things about people, and Oh. My. Goodness. It was a tough week! Things just slipped out! 'They're annoying', 'You're a geek!', 'I don't like him' — and that was Day 1! I felt like a failure but I was determined to get better at it. It turns out that being kind is tough! Slowly, as the week continued, I said fewer and fewer negative things about people. It took real effort and it's something I had to practise daily.

Lucy's kindness has had a big impact on me, I love the way she loves people and makes a choice to say kind words. How about you? Do you speak kindly about people? Or are you in a bit of a habit of moaning about people and saying bad or nasty things? So my challenge for you today is a simple one but it's going to be tough — choose kind words. And then try again tomorrow, and for the rest of your week, to get better and better at it. It's going to take real effort, but let's practise doing this together. You never know, you might just inspire others around you to do the same.

18 JAN

"

A cheerful heart brings a
smile to your face.

Proverbs 15.13, *The Message*

"

OUR INSTRUCTION MANUAL

If I gave you some Lego and asked you to make a helicopter, would you be able to do it? I'd be completely lost and the outcome would look nothing like a helicopter. However, if you gave me some Lego along with the instructions on how to make a helicopter, I'd love following the steps to create it.

For me, the Bible is my instruction manual; it's my guide for life. When I'm not reading it, I feel lost, and as though I'm just not on track. However, when I read it, I feel I'm able to see things more clearly and know which step to take next.

I believe that the God who created the universe, who lovingly created you and me, can speak to us through the words of the Bible. It's a book full of wisdom and hope, which I believe can guide us in every situation and circumstance. In fact, in the Bible God actually promises that it will be a 'lamp for my feet, a light on my path' (Psalm 119.105).

Sometimes it's hard to know where to start when reading the Bible. Do I start at Genesis or Matthew? Do I just randomly open the book and pick a verse? If that's something you struggle with, here are three places to start with:

- Old Testament – Isaiah 43.2
- Psalms – Psalm 91
- New Testament – Colossians 3.13.

20 JAN

God, I trust you
with all my heart.
Please lead me
and I will follow.

21 JAN

LOVING OURSELVES

What words would you use to describe yourself?

Someone once asked me that, and I could think of far more negative words than positive ones. I remember, when I was younger, reading a book by Beth Redman where she writes about her daughter Maisie running around the house singing, 'I love me, I love me!' That stuck with me because I don't think I've ever really thought, 'I love me' — have you?

Loving ourselves is often a challenge because:

1. We compare our bodies, our external selves, to those of others. It's hard to love ourselves when we feel our bodies are imperfect, a project to be worked on. We can spend years of our lives, and thousands of pounds, trying to correct ourselves and live up to a standard presented to us by the beauty industry.
2. We know our internal selves. We know deep down that we've said, done and thought things that we shouldn't. We know that we're flawed (we often forget that everyone else is too!). We're imperfect — the Bible calls that sin. Sin is doing wrong and missing the mark; imagine firing an arrow at a target and missing the very centre. *We* know where we've missed the mark, and we hold on to that, finding it very difficult to love ourselves.
3. We carry shame with us. Shame is a powerful and painful feeling centred around how we see ourselves. We can have a negative view of ourselves because of something that's been done to us, or something we have done ourselves. Shame is a heavy weight to bear.

If, like me, you often focus on the times you've messed up, or if the view you have of yourself is a negative one, then pray this with me today . . .

Father God,
I am sorry for the things that I've done wrong
(share those things with him if you can name them). Please forgive me.
Help me to see myself as you see me today,
your beautiful daughter whom you love.
Amen.

22 JAN

Here I am! I stand at the door and knock. If anyone hears my voice and opens the door, I will come in and eat with that person, and they with me.

Revelation 3.20

WHAT IS LOVE?

Love never gives up.
Love cares more for others than for self.
Love doesn't want what it doesn't have.
Love doesn't strut,
Doesn't have a swelled head,
Doesn't force itself on others,
Isn't always 'me first,'
Doesn't fly off the handle,
Doesn't keep score of the sins of others,
Doesn't revel when others grovel,
Takes pleasure in the flowering of truth,
Puts up with anything,
Trusts God always,
Always looks for the best,
Never looks back,
But keeps going to the end.

1 Corinthians 13.4–8, *The Message*

24 JAN

I look behind me and you're there,
*   then up ahead and you're there, too —*
*   your reassuring presence, coming and going.*
This is too much, too wonderful —
*   I can't take it all in!*

Is there anyplace I can go to avoid your Spirit?
*   to be out of your sight?*
If I climb to the sky, you're there!
*   If I go underground, you're there!*
If I flew on morning's wings
*   to the far western horizon,*
You'd find me in a minute —
*   you're already there waiting!*
Psalm 139.5–10, The Message

I love this psalm; it makes me feel so comforted knowing that wherever I go God is already there. So remember this today as you walk around, doing all that the day demands: you're not alone.

25 JAN

MY BEST

Today I aim to be my very best,
I won't aim to be better than others,
Not proud,
Or puffing my chest.
And I'm not going to put myself down today,
And I'm going to be kind with the words that I say,
And I'll look out for the people who pass my way.
And whilst I'm trying to be the best that only I can be,
I'll also aim to see
The best in others.

26 JAN

There will never be another you.
You are one of a kind, completely unique
and lovingly chosen by God. He chose you
to be here at this time, on this day, and has a
purpose for you here on earth.

Today, enjoy becoming all that you were
created to be.

I have it all planned out —
plans to take care of you, not abandon you,
plans to give you the future you hope for.
Jeremiah 29.11, *The Message*

27 JAN

Be still, and know
that I am God.

Psalm 46.10

28 JAN

Oh yes, you shaped me first inside, then out;
    you formed me in my mother's womb.
I thank you, High God — you're breathtaking!
    Body and soul, I am marvelously made!
    I worship in adoration — what a creation!
You know me inside and out,
    you know every bone in my body;
You know exactly how I was made, bit by bit,
    how I was sculpted from nothing into something.
Like an open book, you watched me grow from
        conception to birth;
    all the stages of my life were spread out before you,
The days of my life all prepared
    before I'd even lived one day.

Psalm 139.13–16, *The Message*

29 JAN

QUIET STRENGTH

Quiet strength is displayed in getting yourself up in the morning, in telling your thoughts that they're wrong and in putting one foot in front of the other when it feels impossible.

Strength, in this case, isn't muscle-dependent. It's dependent upon training the mind and trusting in God. Quiet strength is knowing that God is with you and that he gives you enough of what you need.

Focus on the day ahead. Don't dwell on yesterday or worry about tomorrow; instead, be present, and focus on the joy of today.

Jessie

30 JAN

An expert in the law, tested him [Jesus] with this question:

'Teacher, which is the greatest commandment in the Law?'

Jesus replied: '"Love the Lord your God with all your heart and with all your soul and with all your mind."

This is the first and greatest commandment. And the second is like it:

"Love your neighbour as yourself."'

Matthew 22.34–39

31 JAN

He's known you from the start
And he's been there all along,
When things have been good
And when everything's felt wrong.
When you've felt like a mess,
Or just didn't understand,
He's called out your name,
and he's reached out his hand.

If you don't know who you are,
Ask him — he'll show you,
Open your eyes too,
Show you the whole truth,
And nothing but the truth.

01 FEB

This is how much God loved
the world: He gave his Son,
his one and only Son.
And this is why: so that no one need
be destroyed; by believing in him,
anyone can have a whole and lasting life.

John 3.16–18, *The Message*

02FEB

AMAZING GRACE

Amazing grace! How sweet the sound
That saved a wretch like me . . .

What is grace? Who's the wretch? And what's he or she saved from?

Grace is getting something you *don't* deserve, and mercy is not getting something you *do* deserve. A wonderful demonstration of this comes from French novel *Les Misérables*.

Branded criminal Jean Valjean has been refused work and shelter but is taken in by a bishop, who feeds him and provides a bed for the night. Valjean steals from the bishop and flees. He is caught and dragged back to confess. Not only does the bishop refuse to press charges, he lets Valjean keep the stolen items and bestows on him a further gift: expensive candlesticks.

The bishop withholds the judgement and punishment Valjean should rightly receive. Sheer mercy. He offers this broken man much more than he deserves. Such grace.

Ephesians 2.8 says: 'God saved you by his grace when you believed. And you can't take credit for this; it is a gift from God' (*New Living Translation*).

Valjean initially struggles to receive the bishop's grace. In the musical adaptation, he sings: 'One word from him and I'd be back beneath the lash, upon the rack. Instead he offers me my freedom.' In the 2012 film adaptation, the bishop is played by the actor who first played the role of Valjean on stage. The symbolism is stark. Having played the character who encountered grace and was brought out of darkness, as the bishop he now offers the next Valjean grace. Valjean's life is utterly transformed and, from that place, he is able to extend grace to everyone he meets.

John Newton, who wrote 'Amazing Grace', used to own slave ships. His life changed when he encountered God, and he eventually helped to abolish the slave trade. He had a deep understanding of his own wretchedness. He knew that his behaviour deserved punishment but that God, in his grace, offered him forgiveness instead.

Like Valjean and Newton, we have all been caught red-handed with stolen goods and been offered the precious candlesticks. How will we respond to this grace and freedom?

Ruth

May the peace of the Lord Christ go with you,
wherever He may send you.
May He guide you through the wilderness,
protect you through the storm.
May He bring you home rejoicing
at the wonders He has shown you.

From *Celtic Daily Prayer*,
Northumbria Community

THERE'S SO MUCH WE'RE DOING RIGHT

Over the past few years, I've realized that I'm not very good at being kind to myself. I regularly have an internal conversation with myself that normally sounds like this . . .

'Oh Meg, you're really not very good at [something], you need to get better.'

That 'something' has been a thousand different things in the past. It's been the little things: replying to people, playing the piano and keeping my house clean. And it's been big things: writing, speaking in public and being confident. As regularly as once a week, I would sit and list all the things that I wasn't doing well.

I knew I had to do something about this pattern of behaviour because it was making me feel rubbish. I decided to make a list of what I'm good at instead. It felt odd to be writing positive things rather than my usual negative put-downs. But do you know what? It turns out there's also a lot that I'm doing right!!

Are you someone who has a habit of putting yourself down? Then will you join me and decide to be kinder to yourself too? It might feel like an odd exercise, but make a list of the things that you're good at and doing well — the big things and the little things. Keep the list and add to it every now and again, and when you find yourself thinking negative things about yourself, take out the list and read through it. Of course, in life there are always things that we can improve on, but I think we need to stop beating ourselves up: there's so much we're doing right.

Do everything in love.

1 Corinthians 16.14

HOME

Where do you feel most at home?

It's been said that home is where your heart is — so it's where the people you love are.

It might be in your actual house, but it also might be with your best friend whom you can be as weird as you like with!

The people who love us unconditionally make us feel at home because there is no pretence. We don't need to be our cleverest, our prettiest or our wittiest — we can just be ourselves because we know we're loved.

We are promised in the Bible that God delights in us and that when he came to us in the person of Jesus he made his home among us — or, in other words, he pitched his tent with us.

If you've ever been camping, you'll know that when you pitch your tent with someone you see people at their worst and their best — morning hair and pre-coffee mood and everything! That's what Jesus does for us and it's why we can feel at home in our own skin.

Rachael

07 FEB

Be on your guard; stand firm in the faith; be courageous; be strong.

1 Corinthians 16.13

08 FEB

WE'RE ON THE WINNING TEAM

I believe that God is love, hope, truth, freedom — in fact, I believe he is everything that is good. But I also believe (and this is something people don't really talk about) that there are forces of darkness and evil. The Bible talks about a fallen angel called Lucifer; he's also been called Satan or the devil. Probably in your head you're picturing a guy in red with little horns and a red tail, right? Yep, we've seen that image so many times on TV and at Halloween that it's almost funny. But what do we know about the devil?

In the book of Isaiah, we read that he was an angel who wanted to raise himself above God...

> How you have fallen from heaven,
>   morning star, son of the dawn!
> You have been cast down to the earth,
>   you who once laid low the nations!
> You said in your heart,
>   'I will ascend to the heavens;
> I will raise my throne
>   above the stars of God.'
> Isaiah 14.12–13

In Matthew 4, it says that he tempted Jesus in the desert, and in John 8.44 it says, 'He is a liar and the father of all lies.'

In 1 Peter 5.8, it says, 'Be alert and of sober mind. Your enemy the devil prowls around like a roaring lion looking for someone to devour.'

That might sound frightening, but the devil is not someone we need to be afraid of, as God offers us his protection. It's good to be aware and on guard, staying as close to God as we can. I love the verse in John 10.10 where Jesus says this: 'The thief [devil] comes only to steal and kill and destroy; I have come that they might have life, and have it to the full.' God is greater and more powerful than the darkness — we're on the winning team!

09 FEB

You've always given me breathing room, a place to get away from it all, a lifetime pass to your safe-house, an open invitation as your guest.

Psalm 61.3-4, *The Message*

MARCH ON

Whatever you're going though, wherever you are,
whatever has happened in the past, march on,
keep going and never give up.

Know that you are enough, just as you are.

You are talented even if you don't see it.

You are beautiful even if you don't believe it.

You are not alone even if you think you are.

11 FEB

He mends my
heart when it
is broken.

12 FEB

WE ARE ENOUGH

The world says we aren't clever enough, pretty enough, thin enough, rich enough. Yet the world also says we're too loud and we're too insecure. It's a paradox of our perceived insignificance.

We always want to be 'prettier', 'smarter', 'thinner' and the danger of these words is the 'er' part. But what if we were to wake up every morning deciding to be the best version of ourselves, rather than seeing ourselves as not good enough? I wonder how that would change our mindset and perspective?! Imagine how much more confidence we would have to do so many more things.

We are not 'too this' or 'too that'. We are enough. But we have to believe that we are enough.

When God looks at us, he knows our failures and our mistakes, but he's a God who still sees us and says, 'My beautiful child'.

He says: 'You are enough because of who you are and I created you exactly that way. Don't waste time being sidetracked by looks: they will only fade over time and they won't fill that empty void within you. You'll never have enough of the worldly things because there are so many distractions and temptations, and they won't satisfy you anyway. But be secure in knowing that I am enough for you. I will not let you down. You can trust my love.'

Allow God to fill you with his love today.

Jessie

Become
friends with God;
he's already a friend
with you.

2 Corinthians 5.20, *The Message*

TAKE THE VERY NEXT STEP

Waiting can often be frustrating, can't it? Waiting for the bus, waiting for people, waiting for a delivery to arrive – yep, waiting can certainly be frustrating a lot of the time. And so it's no doubt that so many people find themselves impatiently wanting to rush through every stage of life so that they can be who they're 'meant' to be right now.

But waiting is actually a huge part of that process. In fact, there may well be certain things you're going through *right now* which are going to help you to become the person you're going to become in the future. There are certain steps which we're not actually *supposed to* fast-forward. Trust the process.

God is sometimes described as being like a commentator at a football match. He can see every player, he can see what is and isn't working, and he can see the entire pitch. Whereas the players, of course, can only see what's in front of them and a few metres around them. They don't have the same perspective as the commentator.

Right now, you might only see what's going on around you. You might question how things are ever going to change and how you're ever going to become that person you know you've been created to be. Try and remember that you don't *need* to have every single step already mapped out – that's God's job. Your job is simply to take the very next step in front of you and trust that, even when it feels small, it's part of a bigger plan.

Naomi

15 FEB

He will cover you with his feathers, and under his wings you will find refuge.

Psalm 91.4

OPEN YOUR HANDS

Recently, I had to spend some time in hospital, and it was probably the most scared I've ever been in my life.

Four months after I'd come home, I was talking to my friend about the ordeal and all of a sudden I started crying. It became uncontrollable; I simply couldn't stop. I started to share about the fear I'd experienced sitting alone in the hospital at night. I recalled the noise of the ambulance siren playing over and over in my head, the smells of the hospital, the beeping of the machines around me and the uncertainty of not knowing what was going to happen. Until I started sharing about it I had no idea how much it had affected me.

I realized that I had bottled up a lot of the feelings that I had experienced, and I'd buried them down deep because they were so painful. It hurt to talk about what I'd been through but I felt a real release in doing it. Now when I feel as though I'm having a flashback or having anxious thoughts about what happened, I speak with my friends and family and release the pressure once more. Praying about it has also helped. God wants us to tell him how we're feeling and promises us peace: 'Peace I leave with you; my peace I give you. I do not give to you as the world gives. Do not let your hearts be troubled and do not be afraid' (John 14.27).

Do you have a painful memory that you're burying deep? Please don't keep the problem bottled up. I know it's incredibly hard, but slowly release the pressure and share your thoughts and feelings with those around you that care – God, your family, a friend or teacher that you trust.

Open your hands and let go.

17 FEB

MY CREATOR CALLING: PART 1

There have been times when I've felt like I'm in a tunnel,
And it's dark and I can't see ahead.
And I'm not getting out of this tunnel,
So I stop and I sit down instead.

And slowly I get used to this darkness,
It's just how my life will be from now on.
No happiness here in the tunnel,
No breeze, no sunrise, no birdsong.

And all I feel is isolation,
I'm here alone as the tears fall down
My tearstained cheeks have been stained for weeks,
In my tears I've wished I could drown.

But in the distance I hear a voice call out —
'My child, lift your head.
I offer you peace and freedom today,
Rise up from this hopeless bed.'

My body feels weak and weary,
but I must respond to the call,
So I lift my eyes and look ahead
and discover I'm not alone after all . . .

In the darkness, I can see others,
Some stumbling, some in a heap,
And all the while I hear the call
'I am close to those who weep.'

MY CREATOR CALLING: PART 2

'Rise up! I'm bringing you back to life.
I'm giving you back your breath.
I'm offering you hope in abundance,
I'm saving you from death.'

So I choose to move my rattling bones,
And slowly hold out my hand,
And I'm filled with a peace I've never known
which gives me the strength to stand.

Now I'm back up on my feet
Hope is rising again, once more.
And I take my first few steps
And I help others from off the floor.

I discover it was my Creator calling,
He's cheering and leading me on.
He wants to show me the sunrise,
feel the breeze and hear the birdsong.

And for the rest of my days I'll pursue my Creator,
Whose words are a lamp for my feet.
He's given me breath so I thank him
And I can't wait for the day that we'll meet.

19 FEB

THE ARMOUR OF GOD

There's a guy in the Bible called Paul who was radically changed by God's love — he went from killing people who followed Jesus to becoming a follower himself! (If you want to read about this awesome change, you can find it in Acts 9.)

Paul writes this amazing letter to a group of Christians in a place called Ephesus, which was an ancient Greek city. In his letter, he says this:

> *Finally, be strong in the Lord and in his mighty power. Put on the full armour of God, so that you can take your stand against the devil's schemes. For our struggle is not against flesh and blood, but against the rulers, against the authorities, against the powers of this dark world and against the spiritual forces of evil in the heavenly realms. Therefore put on the full armour of God, so that when the day of evil comes, you may be able to stand your ground, and after you have done everything, to stand. Stand firm then, with the belt of truth buckled around your waist, with the breastplate of righteousness in place, and with your feet fitted with the readiness that comes from the gospel of peace. In addition to all this, take up the shield of faith, with which you can extinguish all the flaming arrows of the evil one. Take the helmet of salvation and the sword of the Spirit, which is the word of God.*
> Ephesians 6.10–17

When you first read Paul's words, it's easy to think that they don't really apply to us because our daily lives don't look like a battle. But Paul teaches us that as followers of Jesus there's a darkness that we fight against: that darkness is evil and sin. So, over the next few days, we're going to chew over this part of Paul's letter, where he encourages all Christians to daily put on different aspects of the Christian faith, just like pieces of armour, before going into battle!

20 FEB

THE BELT OF TRUTH

In battle, the Roman soldier's belt held everything together; it carried equipment, swords and arrows and was absolutely essential. Just as a soldier would be lost without his belt, so would we be lost without truth. Truth holds everything together, just like the belt.

This analogy made me laugh, but I found it quite helpful as well, so I'll share it . . .

If a soldier didn't have his belt on, his armour would fall down (and he'd be flashing his pants) which would mean he might trip over – and that's dangerous! His belt is important to hold everything in place. Similarly we need to know the truth about life: we need to know the reason for existence and the truth about God, otherwise we can easily trip up.

We read in the Bible that the devil uses lies against us like a weapon; it actually says that he is 'the father of lies'. Throughout your walk of faith he will try many times to deceive you in an attempt to distract you from God. And you will encounter people who will claim to know the way to live a full life, but Jesus said this: 'I am the way and the truth and the life. No one comes to the Father except through me' (John 14.6). This truth that Jesus talks about holds everything together, just as the belt holds the armour in place.

So when Paul talks about the belt of truth, he's getting us thinking about the truths of God and challenging us to apply them to our lives, so that they hold us together.

As you read the truths of God throughout this book, tie them around your heart and, just like a belt, carry them with you everywhere you go today.

21 FEB

THE BREASTPLATE OF RIGHTEOUSNESS

'Righteousness' sounds such a grand old-school word, but the way I like to remember it is *right-with-God-ness*. The only way to be right with God is by believing that Jesus died on the cross, and by his perfect blood being spilt, he purchased that right-with-God-ness for us. We are washed clean by his perfect sacrifice, and when we receive that forgiveness we can come into a relationship with God.

So when Paul talks about putting on the breastplate of righteousness, he's challenging us to totally receive that forgiveness and walk in a close relationship with God. In battle, the breastplate would have covered the chest and protected the heart, and this reminds me of a great verse in Proverbs:

> *Above all else, guard your heart,*
> *for everything you do flows from it.*
> Proverbs 4.23

Satan often attacks our heart — our self-esteem and our confidence. Even though he attacks us and tries to wear us down, we are saved! We have given Christ our sin and he gives us his righteousness. There's an exchange that's taken place, a beautiful exchange.

So defend your heart! Don't believe those lies that he whispers in your ear that you are not right with God, that God hates you or that you should live with guilt and shame. He might even be convincing you that God will reject you in the end for something that you've done wrong but, as we said yesterday, he is a liar! Yes, you are a sinner, we're all sinners. But you can say with confidence, 'Yes, I am a sinner, but I gave my sin to Christ, and he has given me a perfect right-with-God-ness. I have confidence that this breastplate of righteousness will keep me safe.'

22 FEB

THE SHOES OF THE GOSPEL

I was running around the garden at the age of seven when I stepped on a wasp or a bee or something nasty and, oh my gosh, I remember the pain of the sting.

That's the reason you'll never catch me barefoot in the garden. Even in the height of summer, I'll always wear shoes outside. That way, I can walk around without being fearful of what's lurking in the grass waiting to sting me.

The shoes of the gospel are to be worn so that wherever we walk we are secure, walking without fear of what's around us. The 'gospel' is the good news about Jesus, the fact that he's rescued us from the sting of death. It says this in 1 Corinthians:

> 'Where, O death, is your victory?
> Where, O death, is your sting?'
> The sting of death is sin, and the power of sin is the law. But thanks be to God! He gives us the victory through our Lord Jesus Christ.
> 1 Corinthians 15.55–57

Death has lost its sting!! We don't have to be afraid as we walk through life as whatever we encounter, whatever challenge, heartache or trauma, our Father God is with us every step of the way. Once we have discovered this truth of the good news, which can transform lives, it's our responsibility to share it with others and invite them to know Jesus too. Don't be frightened to share your faith — it may be ridiculed and, yes, you might be laughed at, but some people might discover the truth! How great is that! Put those shoes on today.

23 FEB

THE SHIELD OF FAITH

In Hebrews, it says, 'Now faith is confidence in what we hope for and assurance about what we do not see' (11.1). And the dictionary defines faith as 'complete trust and confidence in someone or something'.

Paul says, 'In addition to all this, take up the shield of faith, with which you can extinguish all the flaming arrows of the evil one' (Ephesians 6.16).

My brother is a riot policeman, and he uses a shield so that when he's in the middle of a riot, it protects him from flaming bottles, bricks and other things that are thrown at him. In preparation for riots, he's had to practise using a shield, and he's learnt how to hold it so it best protects him. Without his shield, my brother is vulnerable and open to attack; he could be seriously hurt or maybe even killed. Without our faith in Jesus we are open to attack; we hold up our faith like a shield as we journey through life. And just like using a shield, faith takes practice too!

So when Paul challenges us to hold our shield of faith it means being confident that God is who he says he is and trusting him to keep his promises.

My brother doesn't need to turn and run because he has complete confidence that his shield will protect him. When we put our trust in God, we don't need to be afraid of the devil's schemes or what people can do to us. We can be entirely confident that our Father shields us and holds all our days in his hands.

Your faith might feel small and weak, but the One you put your faith *in* is strong! Remember that today.

'He will cover you with his feathers, and under his wings you will find refuge; his faithfulness will be your shield and rampart' (Psalm 91.4).

24 FEB

THE HELMET OF SALVATION

Salvation means freedom from our sin (the bad things we do). When we give our life to God, we still make mistakes — that's human nature — but God is in the business of changing us and helping us to make good choices. In battle, the helmet protects the head and, if we let God, he'll renew our minds — 'Do not conform to the pattern of this world, but be transformed by the renewing of your mind' (Romans 12.2).

Now imagine a soldier getting dressed for battle. She puts each piece of her armour on, but instead of picking up her helmet she reaches down to the ground, picks a flower, places it in her hair and marches on to the battlefield. The flower looks beautiful but, sadly, it's not going to save her.

That flower represents 'doing good'. Many people believe that by doing good things they'll be saved and go to heaven. The Bible tells us that this isn't actually the truth: there is only one way to heaven and that's by accepting Jesus' sacrifice and giving your life to God. This is called salvation.

Only God can save us. We can't earn salvation by good works — it's a free gift that he offers us, but we have to choose whether to accept it or not. 'But God's gift is *real life*, eternal life, offered to us by Jesus, our Master' (Romans 6.23, *The Message*).

25 FEB

THE SWORD OF THE SPIRIT

Here Paul tells us to carry with us 'the sword of the Spirit, which is the word of God' (Ephesians 6.17).

Jesus battled against the devil in Matthew 4.7. Every time the devil tempted Jesus to do something he shouldn't, what did Jesus defend himself with? The word of God! Check this out . . .

The devil began:

> 'Since you are God's Son, speak the word that will turn these stones into loaves of bread.'
> Jesus answered by quoting Deuteronomy: 'It takes more than bread to stay alive. It takes a steady stream of words from God's mouth.'
>
> For the second test the Devil took him to the Holy City. He sat him on top of the Temple and said, 'Since you are God's Son, jump.' The Devil goaded him by quoting Psalm 91: 'He has placed you in the care of angels. They will catch you so that you won't so much as stub your toe on a stone.' Jesus countered with another citation from Deuteronomy: 'Don't you dare test the Lord your God.'
>
> For the third test, the Devil took him to the peak of a huge mountain. He gestured expansively, pointing out all the earth's kingdoms, how glorious they all were. Then he said, 'They're yours — lock, stock, and barrel. Just go down on your knees and worship me, and they're yours.'
>
> Jesus' refusal was curt: 'Beat it, Satan!' He backed his rebuke with a third quotation from Deuteronomy: 'Worship the Lord your God, and only him. Serve him with absolute single-heartedness.' The Test was over. The Devil left. And in his place, angels! Angels came and took care of Jesus' needs.
> Matthew 4.1–11, The Message

We can learn a lot from Jesus' example here. His weapon of choice? The word of God. God's words hold the power to defend us, to change us and to heal our hurt and sickness. So let's not just read God's words in the Bible, let's learn them! That way we bring God's power into the situations in our life that really need it — like when we're tempted the way Jesus was.

26 FEB

STAND IN CONFIDENCE

Over the past few days, we've been looking at the armour of God. Has it challenged you? What might God be speaking to you about through Paul's words?

When I was younger, I remember someone pointing out to me that as you read through the armour of God, you realize there is nothing mentioned here to protect the soldier's back. My friend pointed out to me that it teaches us we shouldn't turn and run, because then we're vulnerable. So, remember today to stand in confidence, unafraid. You can trust in a great and loving God who is right behind you.

27 FEB

I have loved you
with an everlasting
love; I have drawn
you with unfailing
kindness.

Jeremiah 31.3

28 FEB

BE HER FRIEND

On my first day of Year 7, my mum said to me, 'Look out for the person who looks as though she needs a friend, and be her friend.' Isn't that brilliant advice? It's something that my mum seems to live out — she's such a caring, loving person who supports others.

I wanted to pass on my mum's words to you because I think they're incredibly important — can you be a friend to someone who needs it today?

29 FEB

'B' FOR BIG,
'B' FOR BEAUTIFUL

Just as the photo was being taken, he pointed to me and said, 'It's like the BFG standing at the end of the row.'

The BFG, for those of you who haven't read the book, is the 'Big Friendly Giant'. I'd always hated being tall, but that day I wanted to shrink down and disappear, I didn't want to be a 5ft 9in giant. From that day forward, I developed a habit of bending my left knee slightly when I stood with people, aiming to look shorter.

Over the years, my knees started to get incredibly painful and I've had to have physiotherapy on them, which means I can't do my knee trick any more. I've had to re-learn how to stand up straight and it's a conscious decision I have to make each time I stand still.

I've been in a battle with myself for many years, but my height makes me who I am — it's a beautiful part of me. It's taken me a long long time to accept that.

Are there parts of your body you're ashamed of? Are there things that people have said that have made you dislike yourself? Here's the truth — you are beautiful. Completely and utterly breathtakingly beautiful. It may be a truth that is hard for you to grasp and believe, but that doesn't make it untrue.

Today I want you to think about the way you see yourself. Are you battling against yourself? Like me, are you bending your knee, hiding away? Today, consciously decide to stand up tall and allow the real you to rise up and come out into the open.

01 MAR

You're here to be light, bringing out the God-colors in the world. God is not a secret to be kept.

Matthew 5.14, *The Message*

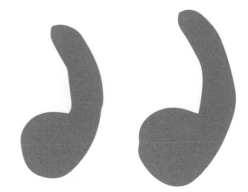

02 MAR

BACK TO LIFE

They say: our bones are dried up and our hope is gone . . . This is what the
LORD says: 'I will make breath enter you, and you will come back to life . . .
I will put my spirit in you, and you will live.
Ezekiel 37.11–12, *New Living Translation*

Are you feeling hopeless, lifeless and breathless? Today, right where you
are, take a deep breath in and fill your lungs with the love of God, your
heavenly Father. And like oxygen, may his love flood through your body,
bringing you back to life. A life worth living.

03MAR

Always be humble and gentle. Be patient with each other, making allowance for each other's faults because of your love.

Ephesians 4.2, *New Living Translation*

04 MAR

A YES HEART AND A YES LIFE

In Luke 1.26–38, we read of when Mary the mother of Jesus is first told that she will give birth to God himself. When the angel appears to her, she is at first troubled, then she has questions and then she simply says: 'I am the Lord's servant . . . May your word to me be fulfilled' (v. 38).

What simple faith. What stunning obedience. *With her heart, with her mouth and then with her life she said yes.*

God is looking for a yes heart and a yes life. We can think this will mean huge sacrifices and doing unthinkably scary things. Although we are told that following Jesus is about denying ourselves and taking up our cross (Mark 8.34), so often this looks like simple obedience in the everyday choices we make. Choices to honour him, to show kindness to others, to step out in faith when we sense him speaking

What might this look like in your life?

- If you know there is something God has been asking of you, through the Bible or by his Spirit, and you haven't been doing it, start by saying sorry.
- Ask him for his courage to do it.
- Ask a trusted friend to pray for you and encourage you to go for it!

Let's choose to have a yes heart and live a yes life.

If you have time, why not read the stories of Esther and Ruth in the Old Testament. They are also great examples to us of women who had a 'yes' in their hearts and in their lives.

Ali

05 MAR

When I awake,
I am still with you.

Psalm 139.18

NEW AND BEAUTIFUL THINGS

In the New Testament, Paul talks about how we need to 'put off' old things in order to step into freedom. The Greek word for 'putting off' is one that expresses real physical effort, like shifting a heavy sofa or redecorating a house. It requires real effort to change your mind, feelings, ways, actions, future and expectations. But it's necessary, and the great news is that we never have to do this on our own. God never abandons us. So what are some of the things you would like to 'put off'? See if any of these resonate with you:

- You've got so good at accepting the lies people say about you that you don't know if you will ever be able to believe anything different.
- You just don't know what you're supposed to be doing. People around you seem so sorted, which is making you retreat into your shell.
- You started masturbating because you were curious about your body and sexual feelings, but now you indulge in it so much that you don't think you can stop. The guilt is weighing you down.
- Past failures are making it difficult for you to step out of your comfort zone and give new things a try. People think you're cynical, but you're not. You're just afraid.
- Your love of fashion has become an obsession. People think you're vain, but you're not. You're just insecure.
- When you feel unable to control or cope with something, you find ways to hurt yourself.
- Someone you love is struggling, and you can't fix it for him or her. It feels like a heavy weight around your neck, and makes you question your ability to love.

If you're in one of these places now, or they are where you sometimes find yourself, remember that Jesus is really good at finding us when we feel lost. And more than that, he's incredibly good at making new and beautiful things out of lives that feel trapped. He's the Master of new beginnings and fresh hope.

Rachel

07 MAR

THE DARK SIDE OF THE INTERNET

A friend of mine (we'll call her Amy) is 13, and she told me a story of something that happened at a sleepover she went to. The girl whose house the sleepover was at decided to enter a chat room, and pretty quickly live footage of naked middle-aged men was coming up, and these men were touching themselves.

Amy told me it really upset her and she asked her friends to stop, but they found it funny and carried on clicking on more.

Amy's experience horrifies me, to be honest, but sadly it's happening a lot. Amy's friends found it funny, but it's not a joke: these people are perverts, predators and paedophiles waiting online, and they want to see you and talk to you. There's a really dark side of the internet which is very dangerous; clicking on videos and entering chat rooms can suddenly become very frightening and can deeply affect you.

There's so much online that we need to stay away from, so please, take care online today.

08 MAR

COMBAT LONELINESS

I heard on the news recently that loneliness is at an all-time high. Apparently there are millions and millions of people, especially older people, who don't speak to anyone from one week to the next. Can you imagine that? Not speaking to a single person for a *whole* week? It made me incredibly sad to think about all those people who feel so alone, and it has challenged me to engage with the older people in my community.

There are practical things we can all do — it could be as simple as saying 'Good morning' to an elderly neighbour or offering to pop to the shops for someone we know might find it hard to get out.
Perhaps you could make a decision to go round and visit your elderly relatives more often.

There are people around you today who need to know that there's someone who cares. Can you be that someone? Let's make a choice to give our time and combat loneliness.

09 MAR

God always meets us where we are and slowly moves us along into deeper things.

Richard Foster,
Christian theologian and author

FINDING A GOOD RHYTHM

As you're reading this, I can guess you're one of two types of people when it comes to getting stuff done. You might be in the group of those who are always on time when it comes to deadlines — the type who actually get things done early and are one step ahead. Or you might be the type to leave things until the very last minute before a deadline and then panic that you don't have enough time to get things completed.

As much as it pains me to admit it, I'm very much the latter. This is a habit I do try to break myself away from, though. The Bible talks about the importance of hard work and speaks against being lazy (I guess procrastination is a form of that!). Because, the truth is, being able to be proactive in getting things done is such a good habit to take hold of. It means you actually give yourself more time, more space to think and plan, more opportunity for rest and relaxation — especially mental rest and relaxation.

Just think about that last pointer for a moment — mental rest and relaxation. Think about the last time you chose to put something off until the last minute. How did it make you feel? If you're anything like me, it would have taken up a lot of headspace! Imagine how freeing it could be if you were able to stop rushing from deadline to deadline in a frenzy, and instead were able to find a good rhythm. That takes practice, but why don't you start today? Is there anything lingering in your mind that you've been putting off? Why don't you spend some time getting it done today, and free your mind up to rest?

Naomi

11 MAR

Let the morning bring me word
of your unfailing love,
for I have put my trust in you.
Show me the way I should go,
for to you I entrust my life.

Psalm 143.8

12 MAR

TAKE CARE OF YOURSELF

Has anyone ever told you how precious you are? I love that word, 'precious'. The *Oxford English Dictionary* defines the word as: 'Of great value; not to be wasted or treated carelessly.'

How are you treating yourself? Would you say you're looking after yourself or wasting yourself? We can't be careless with our bodies, our hearts or our minds.

So, what does it look like to look after ourselves? Here are a few ideas:

Drinking enough water, giving ourselves enough sleep, eating enough fruit and vegetables, learning to accept compliments, praying, not saying negative things about our bodies, not looking at explicit images online, forgiving people, protecting our skin from the sun, laughing, unplugging from technology (once in a while!), not drinking too much alcohol, learning not to compare ourselves with those around us, doing exercise . . . I could write 100 more but these are definitely some things to be thinking about. Can you think of any others?

Is there anything in that list that jumps out at you? Keep it in mind today and take care of yourself — you are incredibly precious.

Life will be brighter than noonday,
    and darkness will become like morning.
You will be secure, because there is hope;
    you will look about you and take your rest in safety.

Job 11.17–18

*14 MAR

ARE YOU *REALLY* LISTENING?

One of my friends, Sarah, remembers things. Let me explain . . . She will say to me, 'How was that meeting of yours last week?' and I'm always so surprised that she's remembered a small detail of my life. Sarah listens to me – she chooses to remember what I've said and then will check in with me. How lovely is that? It makes me feel so loved and cared for.

So I guess the question I want to ask you, and I think I need to ask myself too, is: are we listening to our friends? Are we listening to what they're *really* saying and do we remember to check back and see how things are?

For example, if your friend makes a comment about her parents arguing, will you remember in a couple of weeks to ask, 'How are things with your parents?', or if your mum makes a passing comment that she's not sleeping very well, will you check in with her a little while later and ask, 'Are you sleeping any better?'?

Pay attention to your friends and family, and show that you really do care about their lives and how they're coping. Remembering the little details of their lives, just as Sarah does for me, will help them to feel loved and valued.

15 MAR

BIG QUESTIONS: DID JESUS REALLY RISE FROM THE DEAD?

Jesus' resurrection is central to the Christian faith, but not everyone believes he rose again. Here are some alternative theories.

He didn't die

Crucifixion was brutal. And even before this, Jesus had a crown of thorns pressed into his head and was flogged with a whip made from metal and bone, which would have ripped his flesh.

In John's account, a spear thrust into Jesus' side produced blood and water (John 19.34), which may indicate blood-clotting in Jesus' arteries, pointing to heart failure and death.

The body was stolen

The Roman soldiers who guarded tombs were more hardcore than Marines. Jesus' disciples would have been in mourning, not eating properly and incredibly weak. Would they have been able to overpower the guards to steal Jesus' body? Most of the early disciples were killed for their faith. If they knew the resurrection wasn't true, why would they be willing to die?

If the Roman or Jewish authorities stole the body, why didn't they produce it to prove Jesus didn't really rise from the dead? If it was tomb robbers, why would they leave the expensive spices and graveclothes and steal a worthless body?

People hallucinated

Hallucinations usually occur among people with vivid imaginations. The disciples don't fit this description. Matthew was a shrewd tax-collector, Peter a tough fisherman and

There is no such thing as a collective hallucination, yet various groups claim to have seen the risen Jesus at the same time (1 Corinthians 15.5).

People lied

In 1 Corinthians 15, Paul names people who saw the risen Jesus and, in so doing, he recommends his readers fact-check with eye-witnesses. If Paul had written a false story, people would have corrected him.

What's the best way to explain the hundreds of people who claim they saw the risen Jesus, the sudden fearlessness of the disciples and the dramatic growth of the early Christian Church? With no convincing alternative, the evidence points to the resurrection. As Sherlock Holmes says in *The Sign of the Four*: 'When you have eliminated the impossible, whatever remains, however improbable, must be the truth.'

Ruth

16 MAR

Trust GOD from the bottom of your heart;
   don't try to figure out everything
      on your own.
Listen for GOD's voice in everything
   you do, everywhere you go;
      he's the one who will keep you on track.

Proverbs 3.5–6, *The Message*

BE CAREFUL WHAT YOU BELIEVE

I saw a photo online recently and thought it was so amazing that I shared it with my family and friends! You might have seen it: it shows some wolves walking in a line through the snow. It basically said that the three wolves at the front were old or sick, and it explained that the whole pack looks out for the sick ones and moves at their pace.

I thought, 'Ahh, that's so lovely!!' and so I sent it . . . to a lot of people. To my embarrassment I started getting replies that were saying, 'Meg, it's not true', 'Haha, that's a hoax', 'FAKE'.

Do you ever wish there was a way of getting back texts that you've sent?? It made me feel pretty stupid, but it was also a really good reminder for me that I can't take everything on the internet as truth — there's a lot of untruth online.

We've got to be careful what we accept and believe from the internet as so much of what we soak up can shape us. Not only are we presented with fake images, we're also exposed to the lies that (1) our lives aren't as interesting as those of the people we see in social media, (2) we aren't as beautiful as the girls with loads of followers and (3) to exist we need to post a photo of everything that happens in our life.

Do you sometimes find yourself believing that everyone else online has a much more glossy and glamorous life? It's not the truth. Just as the wolf photo was not the truth. Now I'm not going to suggest that you leave social media, because I really like it too! But we need to recognize that a lot of what we see has been staged — the lighting, the hours in hair and make-up, the paid promotions. We need to keep reminding ourselves of the fact that we are not seeing the reality of people's lives.

Please don't measure yourself up against something that really doesn't exist.

Be bold, be strong,
for the Lord your God
is with you.

19 MAR

You're blessed when you've worked up a good appetite for God. He's food and drink in the best meal you'll ever eat.

Matthew 5.6, *The Message*

20 MAR

WHERE IS THE LOVE?

The Black Eyed Peas released a song in 2003 called 'Where Is the Love?' that asked important questions about how the world got so messed up. In 2016, *GQ* magazine announced that the band was releasing a reworked version of the song to 'commemorate just how rubbish things have got in terms of global affairs'.

The new music video features numerous celebrities alongside harrowing news footage and victims of horrendous crimes. One lyric asks whether we can practise what we preach and turn the other cheek. Love can be incredibly painful, and we find the ultimate example of this excruciating love in Jesus.

Jesus had numerous opportunities to save himself, yet he chose to die because of his overwhelming love for us. In the music video, Black Eyed Peas bandmate Taboo says: 'If you never know love, then you never know God.' This comes straight from the Bible! In 1 John 4.8–10, it says: 'But anyone who does not love does not know God, for God is love . . . This is real love – not that we loved God, but that he loved us and sent his Son as a sacrifice to take away our sins' (*New Living Translation*).

Taboo also says: 'If you never know truth, then you never know love.' If a stranger says he or she loves me, it doesn't mean anything. How can it be true if this is someone who knows nothing about me? The words 'I love you' are only meaningful if the person speaking them knows the truth about us.

Sometimes we withhold information because we think, if people discovered the truth, they wouldn't like us, let alone love us. Yet God knows the whole messy truth about us and still passionately loves us.

Towards the end of the song, DJ Khaled says that love is the key, the answer and the solution, and that love is powerful. The only reason love can be all these things is because love is a person.

The solution to this messed-up world is for God who *is* love to come and help, and to give us guidance.

Ruth

21 MAR

LOOKING AFTER OUR MENTAL HEALTH

We're used to the idea that we have to look after our physical health, aren't we? Whether it be eating our vegetables or making sure that we get enough sleep, we can take steps to make sure we stay physically healthy.

Did you know that the same is true for our mental health?

While we can't necessarily stop ourselves becoming unwell, there are steps we can take to ensure we're taking care of our mental health, and a lot of the time the things that are good for our physical health are good for our mental health too!

Making sure we get enough sleep, that we're getting outside and getting enough rest are all important for both physical and mental health, but so too are being able to talk honestly about what we're going through and finding different ways to face difficult emotions.

What could you put in place today to make sure you're looking after your mental health?

Rachael

22 MAR

Hungry, I come to You
For I know You satisfy
I am empty but I know
Your love does not run dry

Broken, I run to You
For Your arms are open wide
I am weary but I know
Your touch restores my life
So I wait for You.

'Hungry', Kathryn Scott,
worship leader and songwriter

23 MAR

ENJOY TODAY

There was a period of about three months where I was really struggling. I felt so busy, I wasn't sleeping well, every day I felt stressed and very tearful.

And then my sister bought me a little candle that said, 'Enjoy today' on it. Those words rang in my head so loudly; they played on my mind as I asked myself what it would look like to find some enjoyment in the day, even though the days are tough. I put the candle at the centre of my lounge which meant I saw it 100 times a day.

I decided that, even though the days were tough and I felt pretty overwhelmed by life, I would try to enjoy the day as best I could. I wasn't trying to pretend that I wasn't sad or sleep-deprived but I knew that beyond the sadness there were still great things to be enjoyed — all I had to do was look for them.

I started small — when I ate my cereal first thing in the morning I'd think, 'I'm enjoying this', and when the early morning sun flooded through the window I'd pause to appreciate it. Then when I would walk down the road I'd think about how much I was enjoying the fresh air. Slowly my mindset began to change, I'd enjoy the time spent with family, the hot coffee and cake, the laughter — there really were things to be enjoyed in the middle of the difficult days.

On the days that you feel sad or worried or overwhelmed by situations, remember, you *can* find enjoyment in this day. Please don't think I'm asking you to pretend and hide your emotions; it's so important for you to be real with the people around you. But we could all do with practising enjoying the little things and being present. Why don't you try it today?

For God so loved the world that he gave his one and only Son, that whoever believes in him shall not perish but have eternal life.

John 3.16

25 MAR

I WILL BE WITH YOU

There's a guy in the Bible called Moses, and I've always loved his honesty. God tells Moses he wants him to go and save a group of people called the Israelites who are being held as slaves in Egypt.

And Moses' reply is probably what most of ours would be: 'I am a nobody! How can I go to the King of Egypt and bring the Israelites out?'

God's reply? 'I will be with you.'

Moses pipes up again: 'What if they don't listen? . . . But I'm not a good speaker! . . . Please send someone else!'
God has this huge task for Moses and he's scared. Do you ever feel like Moses? Who am I? I'm no good! Please choose someone else! I believe that God has a plan for all of our lives. Sometimes we can feel scared about where he's sending us and about what he's asking us to do.
    Maybe God is wanting you to do something that you just don't feel ready or prepared for – 'Please choose someone else!'
    What was God's reply to all Moses' worries?
'I am sending you, I will be with you.'
    Moses and his brother Aaron led thousands and thousands of Israelites safely out of Egypt. They were able to save them because (and *only* because) God gave them the ability. God did it through them; they just had to trust him and put one step in front of another.

As the weeks and months go by, I want to encourage you to pray this prayer:

God, I will go and do and say what you want me to;
please give me the courage.
I trust you with all my heart.
Please guide me and I will follow.

Be strong. Take courage. Don't be intimidated. Don't give them a second thought because GOD, your God, is striding ahead of you. He's right there with you. He won't let you down; he won't leave you.

Deuteronomy 31.6, *The Message*

27 MAR

BE AN ENCOURAGER

A couple of years ago, I attended a few events where the pressures on, and expectations of, the twenty-first-century girl were discussed. What struck me most was that we have actually created and sustained a culture where it's become normal to slate and discourage other girls. Competition creeps up from every corner.

Yet Jesus entered into the culture of his time and transformed it by being an encourager. He spent time with the outcast, the lost and the alone. That didn't make *him* outcast, lost and alone. Jesus transformed culture by encouraging all those he spent time with — he totally eradicated negativity when talking to and talking about other people.

We need to support and love one another. We need to be real community rather than virtual community. We need to come alongside those younger than us. We need to fight for one another.

There are countless verses in the Bible commanding us to be encouragers. Let's be countercultural in our approach to other people, knowing that our value is not determined by other people but that we can use our words to make others feel valued.

Jessie

28 MAR

EYES UP, FOCUSED FORWARD

Sometimes we come up against difficult obstacles in our lives — difficult, upsetting or frustrating situations which we find it hard to get over or get around. Sometimes we find ourselves tripping over, bloodied and bruised. We can look up and see others leaping along, with smiles on their faces, like elegant deer. How can they get it right while I can't? Why is it so hard for me?

I don't know what the hurdles are in your life. There may be one or two, or perhaps there are hurdles in front of you for as far as your eyes can see. You may be tired from attempting to get over them, but don't sit down and give up on the race. You won't always feel the way you do today — sad, angry or frustrated . . . it won't always be this way.

Keep your eyes on Jesus.

Take small steps towards each hurdle, eyes up, focused forward. Don't compare yourself to those on your left or those on your right, but move at your own pace. Slowly you'll be able to step gently over a hurdle and make progress.

As you move forward, remember to look out for those struggling and limping over their hurdles too. Make an effort to always be a cheerleader for those who need a little encouragement in their race.

29 MAR

Your peace
Flowing like a river,
You are the peace giver,
You surround me with your arms,
With you I'm safe from harm.

Your love
Covers me gently now,
I'm loved and I don't know how,
I've failed and I've turned away,
But you've stayed, waiting for this day.

Your grace
Offered to me so freely,
You surround me and I sense you near me,
I'm released from my wrongdoing,
My faith is rising, growing, brewing.

Your forgiveness
Bursts forth in my direction,
Cleaning my sin, this infection,
I'm washed, a new creation.
Thank you, Jesus, for my salvation.

30 MAR

BEAUTY THAT MATTERS

There's a lot of emphasis in our culture on beauty and on external appearance. There's a lot of emphasis on how your skin looks, on contouring, on having no pubic hair on your body, on your outer beauty, but there's not a lot of emphasis on your inner beauty coming out.

I think what we tend to call beauty, I would call glamour — glamour is your fashion, it's painting your nails, wearing make-up (and that's great, I'm really into all that! I love it). But I think it's really important that all that stuff is an expression of who you are, not a way of masking who you are.

What I dislike most about the selfie culture is that people take 30 or 40 photos of themselves before they put one up, and what happens then is that you see a perfect image of somebody but it's not the real them. It's not their heart, it's not them being spontaneous and unique and brilliant and a bit kooky: it's yet another perfect face like all the faces in the magazines and it's a little bit soul-less.

We live in a culture that says, 'You need to be this!' but inside we feel as if we're so much more than that. When you take a selfie, just take a couple rather than 30 or 40 and then choose one — try to be more authentic about yourself. It's great to love images and fashion, all that, but also work on who you are inside because it's who comes out of you — that's the stuff that people remember, that's the stuff that makes you attractive, that's the stuff that changes the world.

I think that what leaves the best impression on people is not how good your contouring is or how good your selfies are, but the kind of person you are and how you make other people feel.

Rachel

31 MAR

TIN TOBOGGAN

When I was 14, my best friend Sarah and I went to Switzerland. We visited this metal toboggan run that went down the side of a mountain. After the safety briefing, Sarah raced off first, and when she arrived back she whispered, 'It's so much more fun if you don't use the brake around the bends.'

As I slid into the cart my heart was racing, and I was off! It felt as though I was going at the speed of sound! It was so loud as the metal rushed past my face. As I approached the first bend, I used my brake and whizzed up the side of the run. Suddenly the second bend appeared, and in that split second I decided to follow Sarah and not use my brake. The next thing I heard was a loud bang and everything went dark. Then the pain hit me like a ton of bricks. I had flipped my cart upside down in a tunnel and I was lying on the metal run with my leg trapped.

Shaking with shock, I managed to pull my leg out, climb over the edge and crawl out of the tunnel. I limped and stumbled up the mountain in a pretty hysterical state.

That accident in Switzerland challenged me about being influenced. Sarah was – and is (!) – a lovely person and still one of my closest friends, but even our closest friends can make bad decisions and influence us negatively. So it's down to us to be careful whom we listen to and then ask ourselves questions like: 'Is this sensible? . . . Is this safe? . . . Is this good for me?' I'd have avoided a lot of pain if I'd asked myself those questions.

You don't *have* to do what your friends are doing or are telling you to do. I know it can be hard to say no and stand out from the crowd, but it's so important to look after yourself.

Have you been influenced to do something that you know deep down you shouldn't do? Then today is the day to put the brakes on and protect yourself.

01 APR

It is absolutely clear that God has called you to a free life. Just make sure that you don't use this freedom as an excuse to do whatever you want to do and destroy your freedom. Rather, use your freedom to serve one another in love; that's how freedom grows. For everything we know about God's Word is summed up in a single sentence: Love others as you love yourself. That's an act of true freedom.

Galatians 5.13–14, *The Message*

02 APR

IS THE NEW TESTAMENT RELIABLE?

Questions we can ask about ancient literature

1 *How long after the event happened was it recorded?* If I went to a party last night and wrote a blog about it this morning, my account would be more reliable than if I wrote it in 50 years' time when I'd forgotten all the details.

Some events in the Gospels were recorded within a few years of Jesus' death and resurrection. People who were around during Jesus' lifetime would still have been alive. If the stories had contained exaggerations or wrong information, people would have corrected them.

2 *How much time elapsed between the production of the original manuscript and the earliest copy?* Without computers, ancient literature was handwritten. The less time between them, the more reliable they are.

3 *Does it matter how many manuscript copies exist?* The more copies the better.

The most reliable piece of ancient literature, according to these questions, is *The Iliad* by Homer, which has 634 manuscripts and at least a 500-year gap between the original and the first copy. There are more than 24,000 manuscripts of the New Testament with fewer than 25 years between some and the original.

Questions we can ask about the New Testament

1 *Are there any differences between the biblical manuscripts?* Variations are inevitable given the huge number of copies, but the majority of differences relate to spellings and synonyms. Even atheist scholars agree that no differences affect the essential teachings of the Christian faith. The slight differences between manuscripts actually point to the text being genuine. If they were identical, you'd wonder if there was some sort of agenda to promote a particular (doctored) version.

2 *Are there outside sources that back up the text?* First-century historians Tacitus and Suetonius (Roman) and Josephus (Jewish) confirm many things in the Gospel accounts. Numerous historical artefacts referred to in the Bible have also been found.

As well as evidence beyond the New Testament, there's internal evidence. The Gospel writers have niche knowledge of locations, people and agriculture, which places them within a first-century-Palestine context.

The New Testament passes every ancient literature test, but the real question is: do you believe it's true?

Ruth

03 APR

OUR STORIES

Our stories can offer hope to others amidst their despair. Sometimes the hardest part about going through something difficult, whether it be bullying or parents separating, is that we feel as though no one knows how we're feeling.

When we are honest about what we're going through, whether it be to a parent, a friend or a youth worker, we have a chance to share more about the author of our story – God.

Psalm 107 says, 'All of you set free by GOD, tell the world!' (v. 2, *The Message*). Our stories need to be told because they aren't just our story – they are a part of God's story.

It might be that we share our stories with someone in person, or it might be that we share them on paper or in prayer.

It doesn't matter how we share our stories, it's just important that we do share them.

How could you share your story with those around you?

Rachael

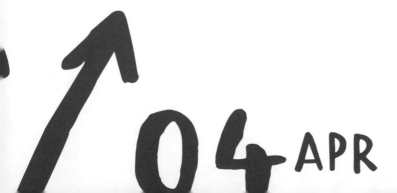

04 APR

Stop beating
yourself up;
you are a work
in progress.

05APR

POST!

I was eating my breakfast the other day and I heard my letterbox go. It was far too early for the postie to come so I wandered to the front door. On the doormat lay a beautiful envelope and inside was a card from my friend Catie. She knew I'd had a bit of an emotional week, and her card was simply to encourage me to keep going — how thoughtful!

I love getting post! Do you? Who do you know that might need an encouraging card or letter? Is there someone you'd like to say thank you to? Grab a pen and paper today and get writing.

06 APR

God is waiting for us. If we choose
to follow him and open our lives up
to his love, we won't be disappointed.

'We throw open our doors to God and
discover at the same moment that he has already
thrown open his door to us' (Romans 5.1–2, *The
Message*).

07 APR

FREE TO BE ME

When you're in a relationship, there are going to be all sorts of emotions that come to the surface — there's a lot of uncertainty, a lot of excitement, maybe some drama. Sometimes the feelings are big and overwhelming, but one of the ways to know whether you're in a good relationship is to ask yourself, 'Do we feel happy in each other's company?'

If we're really honest, one of the reasons that we don't have a good time is where we have to pretend to be who we're not. I remember going out with a guy when I was a teenager; it was quite an intense relationship and he was quite grumpy most of the time, but I thought it was going well. One day my friends said to me, 'Rachel, every time you're with him, you're just horrible, you're on edge and nasty.' They could see that I wasn't free to be me and they could see that when I was with him I was desperately trying to be the person that he wanted me to be. So sometimes we can't rely on our own judgement to find out whether a relationship is good or not. If you're in a relationship, why don't you check in with your friends? It's really good to get the advice of people who really love us and know us well.

Rachel

08 APR

WORDS

When I think about some of the words and phrases others have spoken to me in my life, I always seem to go straight back to the negative words that were said to me rather than the positive ones. Somehow, we have the incredible capacity to return to what hurts us rather than to what encourages us!

During my childhood someone had spoken the word 'shy' over me repeatedly. I realized I had grabbed that mask and worn it for so many years that it started to define who I was and how I approached different situations. But that wasn't me. I realized at that point that we have the power to decide to what extent these words affect us and define us. We have more authority and responsibility than we initially think.

Just because someone says something about you doesn't mean it's true. Not one bit. This is why it's so important to know who we are, inside and out. It means that with any words thrown our way, we get to assess them against what we *know is* true about ourselves, and if it isn't in line with these things then we can scribble it out.

And how can we know what's true about ourselves? By spending time with God, our Creator and loving Father. Ask him today to re-remind you of who he's made you to be.

Jessie

Always look on the
br.ight side of life.

10 APR

BRINGING SHAME INTO THE LIGHT

What's the secret you could never imagine telling someone else? The sin you hope no one finds out about, the part of your life you are most ashamed of? For many years my secret was that I was terrible with money and I'd got into debt. I had credit cards, store cards and an overdraft, and I felt I couldn't tell anyone.

One day I found the courage to tell my friend Liza. I was so embarrassed, afraid of how she might react (even though I knew she was loving and kind), but somehow I managed to get the words out. She was amazing. She didn't judge, she cared, was gentle with me and — being brilliant with money herself — helped me make a plan to start budgeting and get out of debt.

When it comes to shame, we fear we are a bit like a cartoon vampire: if the light shines and our sin is exposed we will turn to ash and die. The reality is that when we expose our sin, our failures and fears it is those things that are destroyed, not us. In true friendship, we are fully known and fully loved. This is how God loves us and how we are meant to love one another.

Who could you be a 'Liza' to? Who can you trust with your secrets? It will take courage but it will bring freedom. Shame thrives in the dark but it cannot survive the light of friendship and love.

11 APR

Trust in the LORD for
ever, for the LORD,
the LORD himself,
is the Rock eternal.

Isaiah 26.4

12 APR

ANGELS IN THE CLASSROOM

When I was 17, my sociology teacher (let's call her Miss T) asked if anyone was a Christian. As I lifted my hand, she stared at me intently and asked, 'So do you believe in angels?'

The question took me by surprise, 'Yes,' I replied. Miss T stood up from her desk, laughed and said, 'Go on, then, get one of your little fairy friends here.' I remember everyone in my class looking at me and I could feel myself going red. 'Go on!' she said, to which I quietly replied, 'I can't.'

She then went on a rant about God, religion and angels. I wasn't really listening because I was just pleased people had stopped looking at me. The moment I stepped out of that classroom I burst into tears; I felt humiliated. Years have passed but I've never forgotten the way Miss T made me feel.

I can actually see now that this moment shaped me and taught me two important lessons:

- *No one should make you feel inferior.* I shouldn't have let Miss T get away with her bullying behaviour. If anyone in a position of authority over you makes you feel embarrassed, upset or scared, you don't have to put up with it. Please tell someone you trust about it and how it's made you feel. No one should be allowed to continue to upset you or do the same to anyone else.
- *It's all right to not understand God.* After that sociology lesson, I questioned God and read the Bible, and it made me realize that I don't understand him — but that's all right! I'm not ashamed of the fact that I don't have answers for everything. But what I *do* know is that the more I pursue God and read his words, the more I discover a love and hope so indescribable, so life-changing, I can't help but have faith that he exists.

So thank you Miss T, you strengthened my faith and taught me that I should never put up with bullying behaviour.

13 APR

Give all your worries and
cares to God,
for he cares about you.

1 Peter 5.7,
New Living Translation

14 APR

LOOK FOR THE GOOD

The other day I had a nightmare of a morning.

I was just walking into my lounge with a bowlful of steaming hot tomato soup and . . . I tripped. It's a bit of a blur, but the next thing I knew was excruciating pain as the boiling hot soup covered my entire hand. I ran to the kitchen and immediately ran my hand under cold water.

I cried. A lot.

I dreaded going back into the lounge, because all I remembered was pretty much throwing my bowl of soup as I fell. I peeped around the door. Oh flip. It was even worse than I thought. In the centre of the lounge (on my new carpet), sat the upside-down bowl, with a soup puddle the size of a dinner plate and bright orange splashes reaching all four walls.

Why did it have to be tomato soup?!!! Why not chicken soup, which is pretty much the same colour as my carpet? Gaah.

I spent the next *hour* soaking, wiping and scrubbing. I've managed to get most of it out but there's this huge orange stain right in the middle; I'm not sure that's ever coming out. I sobbed down the phone as I told my mum all about it. She gave me some advice on carpet cleaning and then said, 'Well, Meg, try to remember that some people would just love to have a carpet.'

At first I thought, 'Oh, don't start that!' I was miserable and not in the mood for thinking about being grateful. But actually, my mum was right. When something has gone wrong or we're having a bad day, thinking about what we have to be grateful for is a really good practice.

You might feel a bit like me and not want to think positively, or perhaps you've *forgotten* how to think positively. It definitely takes practice, but when you're feeling frustrated or you're having a rubbish day, pause and think, 'What can I be grateful for today?' It's about changing our perspective and picking ourselves out of the miserable pit. Or in my case, that soup puddle.

Are you in a pit or a puddle? Choose to look for the good today.

Mercy is your specialty. That's what you love most.
And compassion is on its way to us.
You'll stamp out our wrongdoing.
You'll sink our sins
to the bottom of the ocean.

Micah 7.18–19, *The Message*

HE WANTS THE BEST FOR YOU

Throughout my teens and 20s, I was determined to submit my female sexuality to God. I wanted to be available to him, whether that meant getting married or being single all my life. When I dated a guy, I felt that God was testing me at every turn – and it was a test I was failing. After one particularly physical relationship, I developed a masturbation habit as a way to feel better about myself. I felt miserable, but unable to stop.

Convinced that God was angry with me, I stopped asking him to help me have a healthy view of my sexual awakening. I began to hate my body. I was desperate to find a Christian woman who seemed to have this nailed. But no one seemed up for being real with me. This forced me into thinking I needed to look more than sorted, to hide what was really happening. It took me years to realize that the solution wasn't stopping masturbating. The freedom came when I asked God to show me the unmet needs and desires I was trying to meet by masturbating.

If we believe that our female sexuality is an embarrassing or bad part of us, then we'll try to ignore or deny it. If we believe that our female sexuality is God-given and core to who we are, then we'll be more likely to ask God to help us. A sign of having authentic female sexuality is being able to be thankful and accountable to God for it.

The whole of you belongs to God, including your sexual desires, orientation and hopes. God doesn't own you like a possession for him to use and discard. His sense of ownership of you is about him wanting the very best for you. He knows what's good and right for you, and what will hurt and damage you. He knows that you can honour him in how you express your female sexuality, and he wants to show you how!

Rachel

You are different,
and that's all right.
In fact, it's more than all right,
it's fantastic.

18 APR

GRAB JOY

So often we can be convinced that if we could just change ourselves or our circumstances or our haircut or our wardrobe, we would be happy. We become fixated on a self-improvement programme. The sad thing is that we miss out on so much when we're obsessed with changing this or doing that or meeting the person of our dreams.

Right now, wherever you are, complete and utter joy can be grabbed with both hands. Joy is different from happiness: it's far more than just a nice feeling. Happiness is dependent on circumstances; joy is dependent on the fact that God will always be by your side, loving you. Happiness tends to be a result of things, places and people, but joy is a sense of peace and contentment within you.

Joy is found in knowing that you are loved by your heavenly Father, God. You are his child, who he rejoices over with singing (Zephaniah 3.17) and he knows you better than you know yourself.

19 APR

THE FALL-OUT

We've been friends for years, it's such a shame,
I don't feel like it can ever be the same.

I want to do right and clear the air,
But the words they've said are just not fair.

Our friendship is so very strained
And I feel like I've been wrongly blamed.

I don't want to be kind, I want them to pay!
But I know you call me to live a different way.

I want to tell everyone what they've said!
But you ask me to share it with you instead.

Oh help me to show them your love and care,
When I'm feeling hurt, please meet me there.

When I see them, soothe my pain,
Keep me from anger, extinguish that flame.

So I won't get revenge, I won't plot and plan,
I'll place this all in your loving hands.

Show me God how to be a good friend,
I pray that this fall-out will soon come to an end.

20 APR

COMPETITIVE VS CONFIDENT

Are you a bad loser? Do you think something's not worth your time unless you can be the best?

Your abilities and talents are not dependent on your winning all the time. Healthy competition is good, but needing to always be the best can make you feel unhappy or insecure around people.

Sometimes I think that girls are the worst at this kind of competitiveness. Rather than seeing other girls as a threat, we need to be confident in our abilities and skills and be pleased for other girls when they do well at something. There is nothing more unattractive than jealousy. There is nothing more beautiful than being able to appreciate your own abilities and other people's skills.

It all comes back to knowing that God made and loves us, and letting that give us our identity. Look at these words, written thousands of years ago, about how precious and well designed you are:

> *For you created my inmost being;*
> *   you knit me together in my mother's womb.*
> *I praise you because I am fearfully and wonderfully made;*
> *   your works are wonderful,*
> *   I know that full well.*
> *My frame was not hidden from you*
> *   when I was made in the secret place,*
> *   when I was woven together in the depths of the earth.*
> *Your eyes saw my unformed body;*
> *   all the days ordained for me were written in your book*
> *   before one of them came to be.*
> Psalm 139.13–16

Rachel

21 APR

'If you'll hold on to me for dear life,' says GOD,
'I'll get you out of any trouble.
I'll give you the best of care
if you'll only get to know and trust me.
Call me and I'll answer, be at your side in bad times;
I'll rescue you, then throw you a party.
I'll give you a long life,
give you a long drink of salvation!'

Psalm 91.14–16, *The Message*

22 APR

COMPARISON IS THE THIEF OF JOY

Does it shock you to know that God literally calls you a masterpiece? A treasured possession whom he couldn't be any more delighted with? Well, as shocking as it sounds, it's totally 100 per cent true.

It can be hard to grasp these assurances from time to time, though, can't it? All we need to do is take one quick scroll through the latest on our Instagram feed before we find ourselves feeling small and insignificant. Theodore Roosevelt, a US President, coined a quote I often remind myself of in moments like that. It says: 'Comparison is the thief of joy.' If you've ever compared yourself to anyone before, you'll know exactly what that quote is trying to say.

It was never part of God's original idea to cause us to envy one another — to feel miserable simply because someone else looks/dresses/speaks/writes, etc., better than we feel we do. When it comes to God's design, there is no 'better'. He sees all of us as precious and unique in his sight. Never discredit what you have to offer the world by comparing it with what you think someone else is doing 'better' than you. That's simply a tried and tested method to find yourself feeling frustrated, when actually, God simply wants you to be free to be and do all he desires for you. Embrace this truth today and always.

Naomi

23 APR

Look
for
the
best
in
people.

24 APR

COME TO ME

Recently I was having a bit of a tough time. I shared how I was feeling with my friend Kat and she promised to pray for me. Every couple of days she would text and see how I was getting on (what a gem of a friend she is!).

Then one Thursday morning, when I was feeling particularly emotional, she sent me a message saying, 'When I was praying for you, I couldn't get Matthew 11.28 out of my head, I think it's for you right now.' I grabbed my Bible, found the verse and, right then and there, I cried into my breakfast.

Jesus said: 'Come to me, all you who are weary and burdened and I will give you rest.'

It was exactly what I needed to hear – I felt such a sense of relief, peace and hope when I read it. Jesus offers us rest; all we have to do is ask him for it! That's such good news. The Bible is powerful; I believe it's God's words to us and has the power to speak into, and make a difference to, every situation in your life, and your friends' lives too! Do you know someone who needs support, encouragement, hope today? Why don't you share a verse from the Bible with her or him? (There's plenty in this book!)

If you ask God, he might direct you to a particular verse to pass on!

But for today, perhaps, like me you need to hear it too. Jesus said: 'Come to me, all you who are weary and burdened and I will give you rest.'

25 APR

Guide me in your truth and teach me, for you are God my Saviour, and my hope is in you all day long.

Psalm 25.5

26 APR

KNOW THIS

Society will tell you what to think, who to be, what to wear, what size to fit, how to look, what to say, what to buy and how to live. Read that again, and remember it! We need to be aware of the fact that there are a multitude of voices shouting for our attention.

Society will try to convince you to change to fit the mould of 'beautiful', 'successful' or 'happy', but try to take a step back from the voices, the adverts, the noise, and know this:

You are more than *enough. Right now, just as you are.*

How does this truth change how you might approach today?

27 APR

Truly my soul finds
rest in God.

Psalm 62.1

A POWERFUL CONNECTION

Let's talk about sex.

Sex matters to God. Because he made us and also made sex there is always a spiritual thing (a God moment) going on when people have sex.

Something happens between two people even if they are not in love. If you have sex with someone (even if it is oral sex or just touching each other's body in a sexual way), you are making a powerful connection with him or her. Being casual about what you do with your body means you are being casual about how people are treating your heart. Your heart, spirit and body are very precious, so protect them.

Rachel

The Spirit of God made me
what I am, the breath of God
Almighty gave me life!

Job 33.4, *The Message*

KEEP PUSHING, KEEP HOPING

Now, I'm no scientist, but I've heard that it's a huge struggle for a butterfly to push its way out of its cocoon. The butterfly has to emerge from the smallest of places, something which can take a long time. I once heard a story about a man cutting open a cocoon to release a butterfly from its struggle, but the butterfly lay there, shrivelled and wrinkled, unable to fly. Why? Because as the butterfly struggles, it pushes fluid from its body out into its wings, strengthening them and preparing for flight. The struggle is important.

I'm not going to suggest that your struggles are easy or lovely or something to be enjoyed, but I certainly do believe that as you struggle you are growing and strengthening yourself, just like this butterfly. You may feel in the middle of a very challenging time but keep pushing, keep hoping — this is preparing you for flight.

01 MAY

Be cheerful no matter what; pray all the time; thank God no matter what happens. This is the way God wants you who belong to Christ Jesus to live.

1 Thessalonians 5.17, *The Message*

WHO'S CHEERING YOU ON?

I recently came across a poem I wrote aged 14. It's no Shakespearean sonnet. In fact, it employs some pretty jarring rhymes and is simplistic, implying that once you come into a relationship with Jesus, the struggles of being a teenager disappear overnight.

Unfortunately, life is often messy, painful and complicated. Inviting God into the disarray doesn't make our problems vanish, but it does mean we have someone to hold us in our suffering and walk with us through our darkest moments.

Like many teenage girls, I often hated myself, both inside and out. I battled crippling doubts, self-image issues and unrealistic comparison. But I also had a deep assurance that I wasn't alone.

Even though I often struggled to believe it, I knew I had someone cheering me on from above. I could rest assured that, no matter what I thought about myself, God saw me as his precious daughter (2 Corinthians 6.18). It is from this place that I wrote this poem:

She used to despise herself,
Couldn't bear to see her face.
But now that she's found Jesus,
She's been changed by his saving grace.

She used to hurt herself daily,
To destroy what she hated to see.
But now that she's found Jesus,
Her beauty's been set free.

She used to deny her true self,
And wear a mask to hide it.
But now that she's found Jesus,
He's revealed the girl inside it.

She used to drink too much,
To take her pain away.
But now that she's found Jesus,
All she needs to do is pray.

She used to put herself down,
And destroy what she could have been.
But now that she's found Jesus,
He's restored her self-esteem.

Ruth

03 MAY

JESUS ISN'T A SUPERHERO

Every time my dad used to put me, my brother and sister to bed he would sing us this song:

> *Jesus loves me this I know, for the Bible tells me so.*
> *Little ones to him belong, they are weak but he is strong.*
> *Yes, Jesus loves me, the Bible tells me so.*

It's a song that has been a beautiful reminder to me that we are often weak but he is *always* strong. For as long as I can remember I've been told about this man called Jesus who loves me. While I was a child, I imagined Jesus was a sort of made-up superhero (just without the cape) who went about doing good things. It wasn't until I was 12 that I realized he wasn't a made-up man! The more I've found out about Jesus, the more I've wanted to be like him. He is the most loving, life-giving man ever to walk on this earth; he taught us about caring for others, about forgiveness, about prayer, and at 33 years old he gave up his life to save us.

This love he has for you, it's huge, it's life-changing and hope-giving! It will change the way you feel about yourself and the way you see situations. Today, ask him to fill you with his love and his strength.

04 MAY

Make
today
worth
it.

BIG QUESTIONS: HOW COULD A GOOD GOD SEND PEOPLE TO HELL?

Judgement and choice are important factors to consider when thinking about hell.

Judgement
We often think judgement isn't compatible with a good God, but that's often because we're on the wrong side of judgement! If we've done something bad, we may be judged and punished for it. We don't like this, even if we know we deserve it. However, this all changes when we see injustice in the world.

A close friend of mine was recently falsely convicted of something terrible. His life has been completely ruined as a result. When someone we love has been hurt, we are desperate for justice. It's not loving to stand by and do nothing.

We've got to look at hell in the context of judgement. A God of love *is* a God of judgement. A good God *has* to judge. In *What Kind of God?*, Michael Ots says: 'The alternative [to hell] is even worse: a God who doesn't care about evil or justice.'

Our choice
God doesn't want anyone to experience hell (2 Peter 3.9). C. S. Lewis says in *The Great Divorce*: 'There are only two kinds of people in the end: those who say to God, "Thy will be done," and those to whom God says, in the end, "Thy will be done"' (p. 72).

God says to each of us: '*Your* will be done. You choose.' God doesn't *send* us to hell; we choose it. But thankfully we can be completely certain of avoiding hell as a result of someone else's choice.

God's choice
When Jesus is about to die, he says to God: 'Not my will, but yours' (Luke 22.42). Jesus chooses to give up his own life and experience hell so that we don't have to.

Sometimes life feels so utterly unbearable that people describe it as 'hell on earth'. At the heart of the Christian faith is Jesus' broken and bleeding body. In Jesus, we have a God who chose to join us in our 'hell on earth', to bring us peace in the middle of it and ultimately to bring an end to it.

Ruth

06 MAY

Live generously.

07 MAY

In peace I will lie down and sleep, for you alone, LORD, make me dwell in safety.

Psalm 4.8

08 MAY

TURNING WORRY INTO PRAYER

The truth is, I can be a right worrier.

Often I feel as if my brain is full to bursting with worries about not having enough time, or people being ill, or having too many things to do, or worries about tomorrow. It leaves me feeling completely overwhelmed.

I had a particularly worrying day recently. It was hard to focus on anything with what felt like 100 worries racing through my mind. I had to do something about it. So I lay on my bed with a pen and paper, wrote the words 'Worry List' and began to list the things that were worrying me.

I breathed a sigh of relief when I could see the things on my mind rather than having them whizzing around my head at 100 miles an hour. However, as I read through them, the relief was replaced with feeling completely overwhelmed! Well, at this point I cried, and as the tears poured down, my watery eyes fell upon the words at the top of the page – 'Worry List'. And just then a thought occurred to me, 'What if I'm looking at this all wrong?' I took my pen and scrubbed out the word 'worry' and instead wrote the word 'prayer'.

And then, with tear-stained cheeks, I went through the list sharing each one of my worries with God. I asked him for his peace and help with all that was on my mind, and in the silence of my bedroom I felt his peace with me.

Sometimes we can bottle up what we're feeling inside and exclude God completely from our lives. What's on your mind at the moment? Instead of worrying, why don't you write a prayer list and share your life with God?

PRACTISING THE ART OF FORGIVENESS

Throughout our lives we're wounded by people. Some wounds may be deep, others may be scratches.

Someone once told me this: 'When we don't forgive, it's as if we're locked away in a prison, but the key is on the inside. You can choose to release yourself and be free by forgiving.'

Forgiveness is not saying, 'I agree with what you've done' and it's not pretending we're not hurt. It's letting the bitterness go, about saying, 'I choose to stop picking at this wound you've given me, because I want to heal.'

If you tripped and cut your knee, it would be important to clean your wound and remove any dirt to prevent infection. Forgiveness is like a cleansing, wiping away the dirt and preparing ourselves to heal.

Please don't think that I'm suggesting forgiveness is easy. I find it really hard. When I remember things people have done that have hurt me, I'm suddenly churned up with old angry thoughts and frustrations. In that immediate moment, I have to choose to let it go and ask God for his peace, otherwise I waste my day being caught up in frustration.

The challenge is that, because we can't forget, we must daily practise the art of forgiveness, which means that forgiveness is a lifestyle. But we're often taught the opposite:

- 'Distance yourself from them.'
- 'Give them the cold shoulder.'
- 'Tell everyone what they did.'
- 'Teach them a lesson.'

Whether we realize it or not, we all wound one another; we say and do things that hurt. I don't know whether you feel hurt at the moment. You might feel as though you have a deep wound or maybe you have a fresh scratch. Choose to stop picking at that wound of yours, replaying over and over what's hurt you. Choose to forgive and let yourself begin to heal.

10 MAY

When life is heavy and hard to take, go off by yourself. Enter the silence. Bow in prayer. Don't ask questions: Wait for hope to appear.

Lamentations 3.28–30, *The Message*

11 MAY

That fear that you fear?
It has no place here.

That worry
that's been on your mind,
Today's the day
To leave it behind.

I ask our God
Of love and hope
To release the chains,
To loosen the rope.

To burn the grip
That held you in fear
I ask him to release you
And draw you in near.

You needn't be afraid
By day or by night,
For he is your protection
Your joy and delight.

Go in peace,
Go fear no more.
Christ has set you free,
Of this I'm sure.

12 MAY

LOVE AND BE LOVED

Being a Christian will take courage and discipline. It's no walk in the park; it'll demand that you change and change and change some more, slowly growing into who God created you to be. Following Jesus will cost you: you might be laughed at, ridiculed or worse. You'll have to make sacrifices, you'll have to be determined, you'll be challenged, but with God on your side, you will succeed in this life of faith.

It's not supposed to be easy. The Bible doesn't promise that when we become a Christian we'll face less hardship or pain, but we are promised that we won't walk alone. And when storms come we won't be in over our heads. Keep your eyes fixed on Jesus, who provides all the hope and all the purpose and all the strength we need.

Following Jesus is the greatest adventure, so give it all you've got.

You were born to know your Creator, to love him and be loved by him.

X 13 MAY X X

You have a voice —
your opinions,
your thoughts,
your words
are just as valid as
anyone else's.

14 MAY

FINDING HAPPINESS NOW

'Happiness'. I wonder what it means to you. Think of the word association game and ponder what words come to mind for you. It might be 'fun', 'laughter', 'love', 'holidays', 'freedom' and many other things besides.

When I look back, I know I spent a significant amount of life living for weekends and holidays. I impatiently awaited lying flat out on a sunbed by a pool and soaking up the rays of sunshine that are totally impossible to rely on in the UK. But I'm so quickly learning that happiness isn't to be awaited, it's to be embedded into our life. It is *not* reliant on future things, such as when you have a boyfriend, when you're slimmer, when you earn more money or when you go to university. You can make a choice to be happy in your circumstances *now*.

Spend a few moments thanking God for all the things you can be grateful for in your life, and use this as a springboard for finding happiness in whatever life throws at you today.

Jessie

15 MAY

Give me the ability to see good things in unexpected places, and talents in unexpected people. And give me, O Lord, the grace to tell them so.

Seventeenth-century nun's prayer

16MAY

WHAT'S YOUR IDEA OF BEAUTY?

Yesterday I met a close family friend who is 13; we'll call her Katy.

I held Katy in my arms the week she was born and I've seen her grow from a little girl into a young woman with hopes of becoming a marine biologist. But now, at 13, she tells me that she hates the way she looks and she's considered cutting herself because of how she's feeling.

Katy's idea of beauty is what she sees online. She's surrounded by a world that says it's all about the shape she is, how big her lips are, how defined her eyebrows are. She is told that her value and worth are wrapped up in her appearance.

But I believe Katy's beauty lies in the hilarious laugh she has; it's totally infectious. It's in the way she looks after others. It's in the amazing freckles all over her face that give her so much character. Katy is incredibly kind-hearted and thoughtful, always asking how I am and whether I've had a good week. I will keep reminding Katy that she is beautiful in the hope that one day she will see herself as I do and, more importantly, as God does.

How do you see yourself? Are you always comparing yourself to the girls you see online? It's exhausting, isn't it? Personally, I do not look like the popular girls on Instagram who have thousands of followers, but does that make me any less beautiful? I shouldn't measure myself up against them and nor should you. What if there really isn't anything wrong with your body, but just with the way you see yourself? If you're struggling with the way that you look, pray this prayer with me today:

Father, help me to see myself as you see me.
I've been having negative thoughts about myself; please help me to stop.
Thank you that you have created me beautiful and I'll always remain that
    way.
You know me by my name and I can have confidence in you.

Still, GOD, you are our
Father. We're the clay
and you're our potter.

Isaiah 64.8, *The Message*

18MAY

PEOPLE TO CHALLENGE US

I recently asked someone called Catie to be my mentor, Catie goes to my church, she's ten years older than me and I really look up to her. When I told my friend about asking Catie to be my mentor, he said, 'Why do you need a mentor?' . . . and that's a really good question!

In my mind, a mentor is someone who can challenge and guide you, someone you can meet every month or six weeks or so to explore life together and chat through your progress. A mentor is someone who can advise, support, direct and encourage you as well, which is something I really need as I write, speak and film.

Do you feel as though you could do with some guidance and support? I would encourage you to seek out a woman you trust to meet regularly. It might feel odd to ask her to mentor you, but we all need people to challenge us and help to point us in the right direction in life.

19 MAY

WHERE ARE THE WOMEN?

Have you ever wondered where the girls are in the Bible? You can probably think of a number of guys without too much trouble, but is the Bible a girl-free zone?

No, look a little more closely and you will see many amazing examples of girls who followed God and led his people. Here are just a few:

- Miriam, the prophet and worship leader (Exodus 15; Micah 6.4);
- Deborah, one of the God-appointed leaders of Israel (Judges 4—5);
- Esther, the queen, as brave as she was beautiful, who put her life on the line to save God's people (the book of Esther);
- Ruth, a beautiful example of faithfulness and trust (the book of Ruth);
- Mary, who was given the job of announcing the good news of the resurrection — the most important event in history (Mark 16)!
- Junia and Priscilla, leaders in the early church (Romans 16; Acts 18).

Look just a little more closely at the Bible and see that throughout there are bold, courageous, faithful women who led, served and played their part in God's story.

God has a call on your life too: ways for you to serve him and display his amazing love and truth in both the everyday and the significant. Do you overlook or dismiss yourself? Do you imagine he'll want to work with others, but not you? Don't believe the lie. He is going to join up with you to fulfil his plans in ways you can't even imagine.

Ali

20 MAY

May the Master take you by the hand and lead you along the path of God's love and Christ's endurance.

2 Thessalonians 3.5, *The Message*

IN THE SPOTLIGHT

One day, I was writing in a coffee shop and a lady sat down in front of me with her baby. Directly above them was a spotlight and it lit up the little baby, who was perched on her mum's lap. She was laughing and kicking her legs, and her mum said to her, 'Are you dancing in your own little spotlight?' You know, something about that sentence really made me think.

We live and move and grow under our own little spotlight, but we're not performing for the approval, praise or applause of others. I remember when I was younger I heard someone say that 'we live our life for an audience of one – God'.

Breathe in deeply the breath he gives you, move the muscles he formed and fix your gaze ahead as you stand in your own spotlight before your Father. He is your greatest fan, your biggest encourager, and he watches the performance of your life every day and cheers you on.

Stand before your Father today and, just like that little girl, dance in your own little spotlight.

22 MAY

GLAMOUR VS BEAUTY

If glamour is the blusher painted on your face, beauty is the inner radiance that lights you up from the inside.

If glamour is the outfit that helps you to make an entrance, beauty is your generous heart that means your presence changes the atmosphere.

If glamour is the perfume clinging to your clothes, beauty is the fragrance of your life that lingers long after you've left the room.

God will always be more impressed with your desire for beauty than with your pursuit of glamour. His creativity pulsating through us inspires us to have fun with glamour. But God calls us into the deeper, richer pursuit of building an inner life of hidden beauty that will radiate from the inside out, through our whole being.

When you look in the mirror, look *for* yourself, not simply *at* yourself. Look for love; look for compassion; look for openness; trustworthiness, hope. Look for courage in the face of trouble. Look for peace. Then let others see this beauty too.

The goal of glamour is to make everyone feel envious. The goal of beauty is to make everyone feel loved.

Rachel

23 MAY

Life is fragile.
Handle with prayer.

24 MAY

GOD IS OUR STRENGTH

Sometimes we don't feel strong. We feel exhausted and wrung out, unsure how to face what is coming.

And so we wait.

And in our weakness we can rely on nothing but God's strength.

His power is made perfect in our weakness. When we rest in him, when we stop trying to be strong all the time, we might just find that the God who is our strength meets us precisely where we are weakest. We can realize that we don't need to be strong all the time; we just need to remember to return to the source of all strength. In Psalm 46.1, it says, 'God is a safe place to hide, ready to help when we need him' (*The Message*). Whatever we face, whatever the fight, God is our strength and we can rest in him.

Rachael

25 MAY

You don't have to
be anything other
than yourself today.

26 MAY

You, Lord, are
forgiving and good,
abounding in love to
all who call to you.

Psalm 86.5

27 MAY

REMEMBER THE RIGHT THINGS

Years ago, I remember someone saying to me, 'When someone does something wrong, don't forget all the things they've done right.' What a great thing to remember!

Sometimes when we think about certain people we're consumed by frustration, hurt, even anger, and all we can think about is their bad points (which we've all got!). Is there someone who has upset you or whom you've fallen out with? Today, make a choice to remember the right things that person's done.

28 MAY

You reached out and embraced me,
Without you, I'm flaky,
But now I'm a new person
Because your love completely remade me.
Ever will you be the song of my heart, regardless
Because you are the light of my life that got sparked in the darkness.
In spite of all my failures and mistakes,
My shame and disgrace,
You took my life and covered it with grace.
I know that all my steps are ordered by you
And so I step with confidence because your love is true.
I know with you I'm never left alone,
If in the valley or on the hilltop, my heart's your throne.
I dedicate my life to you, it's not my own,
I'm looking forward to the day when you will take me home.

'Saviour', 29th Chapter, featuring Tim Hughes, worship
leader, singer, songwriter and Anglican priest

29 MAY

Nothing living or dead, angelic or demonic, today or tomorrow, high or low, thinkable or unthinkable — absolutely *nothing* can get between us and God's love because of the way that Jesus our Master has embraced us.

Romans 8.38—39, *The Message*

30 MAY

Who put the gold into the sunshine?
Who put the sparkle in the stars?
Who put the silver in the moonlight?
Who made Earth and Mars?
Who put the scent into the roses?
Who taught the honey bee to dance?
Who put the tree into the acorn?
It surely can't be chance!
Who made seas and leaves and trees?
Who made snow and winds that blow?
Who made streams and rivers flow?
God made all of these.
'Who Put the Colours in the Rainbow',
Paul Booth, songwriter

This used to be one of my favourite songs at school when I was little. I used to love singing it and imagining the stars, the big oak tree and the snow. I know this is a kids' song, but they're questions adults have been asking themselves for thousands of years. Who made this world? And who made us? Surely this incredible world can't be by chance.

The more I look around at this stunning world, the more I can't help but feel that it points to a Creator, a brilliant, intelligent, loving Creator – God, our heavenly Father who created us to know him.

So do you know him? If not, begin to speak and walk with him today – he's so very close.

31 MAY

SURRENDER

I was eating some Love Hearts® the other day (yum!). The first couple said things like 'Text me' and 'You're mine', and then I picked one up that said, 'I surrender'.

I thought, 'That's really odd', because surrender isn't really a very popular word. It makes you think of weakness, submission and losing — a strange thing to be written on a sweet. The word 'surrender' is a battle term and means to stop resisting and submit, giving up everything to the opposition. The person surrendering lays down his or her weapons and gives over control.

Surrendering or submitting to God is much like this, laying ourselves, our desires, our failure, our selfishness and our own plans aside. Surrendering to God is a decision to kneel before a great leader, a faithful friend and a Saviour God and follow him.

There's a great verse in Proverbs that says, 'Trust in the LORD with all your heart and lean not on your own understanding; in all your ways submit to him, and he will make your paths straight' (Proverbs 3.5–6).

God wants the best for our lives, and so surrendering or submitting to him is not something to be afraid of. We have to be aware, though, that as we bow to him, he may ask something of us — to do something or stop doing something. God wants us to surrender every area of our lives to him, not holding back parts and disallowing him access. He wants you to share those deep things that you've hidden away, the things in your mind you're afraid of. He wants to conquer those thoughts that you fear; he wants to reign over those memories that hurt you; he wants to be king over the past and the pain but also king of your future.

Will you allow him access to the secret hidden parts of your life?

What are the areas of your life that you need to release your tight grip on, where you need to hand over control? Surrender to the One who holds you in the palm of his hand, the mighty loving Father.

01 JUN

But even there, if you seek GOD, your God, you'll be able to find him if you're serious, looking for him with your whole heart and soul.

Deuteronomy 4.29, *The Message*

02 JUN

JOY VS HAPPINESS

It's so easy to think that joy's a kind of hyped-up happiness and that it should be a simple formula for Christians; we're promised it throughout Scripture. In the Bible, Nehemiah talks about the joy of the Lord being our strength.

But joy is not the same as happiness — in fact, sometimes joy can be found in the midst of sadness, in our hardest times.

Joy is the knowledge that we are known and loved by the Creator God; it's unshakeable in spite of our circumstances because God is unshakeable.

Joy doesn't rely on us, our friends, our families or even our circumstances.

It relies fully on who God is — and God is the source of everything good.

Happiness can be a fleeting feeling, but joy isn't fleeting: it's solid and unbreakable because that's who God is.

Rachael

KEEP ON KEEPING ON

Keep going. These are two little words I so desperately want to share with you today. They may well be two little words you don't actually want to hear — especially if you've heard them often recently.

But they're so, so important, which is why I've got to share them with you again. Because I *know* it's hard, I *know* it's frustrating and I *know* that everything in you wants to give up and say enough is enough. But there's so much on the other side of what's going on for you right now. In fact, there's actually a lot for you to learn *within* what's going on for you.

The Bible talks about perseverance 'producing character' and character leading to hope. Which essentially means that in choosing to keep on keeping on, you're learning more about yourself, you're learning more about other people and you're learning more about what trial and difficulty even look like. That might not sound like much fun, but the good news is that there's hope on the other side of all that hardship.

So, as much as it's not necessarily what you wanted to hear today and as much as you feel that I'm sounding like everyone else in your life right now, take it as confirmation that you're doing something right as you face that thing that makes you want to throw the towel in. Instead, ask yourself these questions:

1. What can I learn from this?
2. What positive can I take from this? (Even if it's tiny!)
3. What action, which I've previously been resisting, can I commit to taking today?

Naomi

04 JUN

You're blessed when you're at the end of your rope. With less of you there is more of God and his rule.

Matthew 5.3, *The Message*

05 JUN

BIG QUESTIONS: CAN YOU PROVE GOD EXISTS?

It depends what you mean by 'prove'. True proof only exists in maths. Mathematicians can prove $2 + 2 = 4$, but even science requires a certain amount of faith. Scientists have to believe there's order to the world, that things react in a certain way because forces such as gravity are at work.
Lawyers speak of 'proof beyond reasonable doubt'. They can't *mathematically* prove someone committed a crime, but they can build a case using confession, eye-witnesses and other evidence. It is this type of proof or 'argument' that Christians offer when it comes to God. Here are some examples:

- *Moral argument:* we seem to have an inbuilt sense of right and wrong, which points to an internal law and therefore a law*giver*: someone who put that law inside us.
- *Aesthetic argument:* art and beauty point to something beyond us. Francis Collins, a leading scientist, became convinced of God's existence when he saw a beautiful frozen waterfall.
- *Desire argument:* the feeling that there's more to life suggests we don't belong here. In his book *Mere Christianity*, C. S. Lewis said: 'If I find in myself a desire which no experience in this world can satisfy, the most probable explanation is that I was made for another world.'
- *Cosmological argument:* the existence of the universe ('cosmos' in Greek) points to the existence of a God who created it. When the Big Bang theory emerged in the 1930s, atheists tried to dismiss it because it suggested the universe had a beginning. And if it had a beginning, something or someone must have kick-started that process.
- *Design argument:* if a tiny change occurred in the air's gases or the distance between the earth and the sun, life would be impossible. Is everything perfectly in balance through chance? Or could someone have put it together? Consider how complicated humans are. Could this point to a God who designed us? Isaac Newton said: 'In the absence of any other proof, the thumb alone would convince me of God's existence.'
- *Personal experience argument:* ask any Christian how he or she knows God exists and you will hear that person's own unique story and reasons.

Ruth

06 JUN

Give your entire attention to what God is doing right now, and don't get worked up about what may or may not happen tomorrow. God will help you deal with whatever hard things come up when the time comes.

Matthew 6.34, *The Message*

07 JUN

Nothing you wear is more
important than your smile.

Connie Stevens, US actress,
producer
and screenwriter

08 JUN

THE BEST THINGS IN LIFE AREN'T POSSESSIONS

We live in a world that tells us to 'Buy more! . . . Want more! . . . Have more!' Did you know that in an entire day you're likely to see over 3,500 marketing messages? Whoa! That's 3,500! Each one bombarding you with suggestions and fuelling your desire to 'want'.

But I absolutely *love* this quote . . .

The best things in life aren't possessions.

You know, like a beautiful sunset, cuddles with a baby, laughing till your sides hurt . . . none of these cost money but I really do believe they're the best things in life.

I've been trying really hard each day to keep my eyes open and look out for those simple things in life that make me happy. It's surprising, actually: once you make a decision to look for them, you see more and more beauty around you.

I don't know where you are at the moment or how you're feeling. But what I *do* know is that, right now, there are things in your life that you can be grateful for. Let's pay more attention to the beauty in the world around us and look out for the simpler things.

09 JUN

AMAZING BODIES

Have you ever spent some time thinking about how wonderful our bodies are? So often we only see ourselves in a negative way — we're not thin enough, we're too tall, too short, disproportioned, not the right shape — the list goes on. But listen to these facts about our bodies!

- Just one drop of blood contains about 10,000 white blood cells.
- The entire surface of your skin is replaced about 1,000 times in your life!
- Information zooms along nerves at about 248 miles per hour.
- Your ears never stop growing.
- The tongue is covered in about 8,000 taste-buds.
- Stomach acid can dissolve metal.
- You produce about 40,000 litres of spit in your lifetime. Or, to put it another way, enough spit to fill around 500 bathtubs.
- If you live to age 70, your heart will have beaten around 2.5 billion times!

Take a moment today to appreciate just how incredible you are. You are a walking work of art.

10 JUN

You have heard that it was said, 'Love your neighbour and hate your enemy.' But I tell you, love your enemies and pray for those who persecute you.

Matthew 5.43–44

11 JUN

BIG QUESTIONS: WHO MADE GOD?

Look around you. Think about how many 'made' things there are. The smartphone in your hand, the cake you just ate, the bus you took to school earlier . . . the list goes on. If something has been made, then it needs a 'maker'. Your phone was made by the technical wizards at whichever company created it, the cake was maybe made by your gran, and the bus by a team of mechanics. But who made God?

This is an interesting question and an important idea to explore, but asking: 'Who made God?' doesn't really make sense. It's a bit like asking: 'What does red taste like?'

These questions are what philosophers call 'category mistakes'. Red belongs to the 'category' of colours, not the category of flavours. Red doesn't have a taste, it's a colour! The question 'What does red taste like?' doesn't make sense because you can't taste 'red'.

Assuming God exists, what does it mean to be God? God has to be all-powerful, all-knowing and all-present. All-powerful: in order to be God, he must have power over things like the wind, gravity and people. All-knowing: he must know everything; past, present and future. All-present: he must be everywhere all at the same time.

In order to be God, he must also be 'unmade'. If God made us, the universe and everything in it, he has to be bigger, better and cleverer than everything else he has made. If something or someone made God, that person or thing would be more powerful, more knowing and more present than God. This is impossible, because in order to be God he must be all-powerful, all-knowing and all-present! God must always have existed, so he couldn't have been made.

Things that have a beginning need a maker. Your smartphone, that cake and the bus all need a maker. But God had no beginning, so he didn't need to be made.

If God were made, he wouldn't be God. When we ask, 'Who made God?' we're asking, 'Who made the unmade One?', which, let's face it, doesn't really make sense!

Ruth

12 JUN

I'M SORRY

Just as I was leaving the car park yesterday, *bang*, someone drove into the back of me.

I got out of the car to assess the damage but I couldn't see any dents, which was a relief. There was a long queue of cars waiting behind me so I got back in my car and moved forward. Then the guy from behind appeared at my window and said, 'Is there any damage?'

'No,' I replied, to which he casually said, 'That's lucky,' and walked off back to his car.

I was in shock, not that he'd just driven into me but that he didn't say sorry!

I called my mum and told her about the accident and how he didn't apologize, and she said the following: 'Saying sorry is important; it doesn't automatically make everything all right but it takes the sting away a bit. A bit like cold water on a burn — you've still been burnt but water soothes it, much like an apology. Saying sorry is saying that you'll try not to do it again.' (I love my mum's wisdom!)

I spoke to my friend Kat about saying sorry too and she also added her wisdom into the mix: 'When we apologize to God for the things we've done wrong, he never replies with "So you should be!" We say, "I'm sorry," and he says, "I loved you then, I love you now and I will always love you despite all your faults and failures." For me there is great comfort in that and it gives me strength to swallow my pride and apologize to others.'

I love those two different perspectives on saying sorry. Apologizing and admitting our faults is really hard (I find it a challenge!) but it's so important. Is there anyone you need to say sorry to today?

13 JUN

If you work the words into your life, you are like a smart carpenter who dug deep and laid the foundation of his house on bedrock. When the river burst its banks and crashed against the house, nothing could shake it; it was built to last. But if you just use my words in Bible studies and don't work them into your life, you are like a dumb carpenter who built a house but skipped the foundation. When the swollen river came crashing in, it collapsed like a house of cards. It was a total loss.

Luke 6.48–49, *The Message*

14 JUN

GOD OUR FATHER

When I was 11 years old, I took an entrance exam for a prestigious school in my county. As I walked into the exam, I remember hearing some parents say this to their crying daughter . . .

'If you don't pass these exams, you won't get the horse or the computer.'

Oh. My. Gosh!! Poor girl — going into an exam with so much pressure to do well and please her parents. There was no 'I love you, just try your best'. But instead, 'If you do *this*, you'll get *this*, and if you don't, you'll get nothing.' The way they spoke to her sounded cold and heartless, with such intense pressure.

Now I don't know if this girl failed or not, but if she did, the drop was massive with no crash mat of love and understanding to fall on.

The way that our parents treat us can have a long and lasting effect on how we view ourselves. I don't know what sort of environment you've grown up in — whether you feel supported/ignored/cared for/rejected/under pressure from your parents — but I want you to remember you are cared for and supported by God. He promises to be a Father whom you can always depend on and look to for encouragement and support. Why don't you share with God today about your relationship with your parents? Are you thankful for them? Do you find it hard to get on with them? Do you need God to help restore your relationship? Ask him today to be involved in your family.

15 JUN

O Father would you help me to remember
that who I am is enough,
Because sometimes I feel inadequate
and I find those days quite tough?

Will you fill me with peace and confidence
From my toes to the top of my head,
So that instead of disliking the person I am,
I fully accept myself instead?

SANCTUARY

Where is your safe place? When I was little, it used to be in the gap between my bed and the radiator — it was warm and I could snuggle down with blankets and a book for hours on end. I could read uninterrupted and sometimes melt sweets on the radiator! As I've got older, though, I've found sanctuary more in people than in places.

I've found sanctuary in spending time with those closest to me, who accept me as I am. I've also found sanctuary in the time I spend with God. There is nothing I can hide from him and I feel safe knowing that God sees everything about me and still loves me. My greatest sanctuary is found in knowing I'm loved by God — and it's where you can find sanctuary, too.

Rachael

17 JUN

BLESSED ARE THE PEACEMAKERS

In the Gospel of Matthew, it says this: 'Blessed are the peacemakers, for they will be called children of God' (5.9). Well, what does that mean? And how can we bring peace?

A peacemaker is a pretty radical thing to be, because we live in a world where people are falling out left, right and centre. We find ourselves in the middle of fall-outs, and we take sides as our friends have issues with others. We want the people who hurt us to be hurt too, and we go on the attack with our words. We attack by telling everyone what they've done, and if someone has hurt our friends we are angry and protective.

Are you a peacemaker? Or are you someone who loves a bit of drama and gossip?

Sometimes we can stir situations because it benefits us, or we like the drama, or it makes us feel important when people come and tell us gossip. Peacemaking means working to bring people together and to sort out arguments.

Every country of the world has diplomats that represent their countries abroad. The diplomat's job is to work for peace on behalf his or her country. Wouldn't our families, our schools, our streets and our towns be so much happier if there was someone working for peace on behalf of God? *You* can be that person. God is inviting you to join in with the work he's already doing in those places.

A peacemaker is someone who experiences the peace of God and chooses to share it with others. Can you share peace today?

Yes, my soul, find rest in God; my hope comes from him.

Psalm 62.5

19 JUN

STILLNESS AND SILENCE

Here am I, Lord,
I've come to do your will.
Here am I, Lord,
in your presence I am still.

I don't know about you but I find being still quite a challenge! There's always something on the list to get done, isn't there? People to reply to, rooms to clear, friends to meet. I believe, however, that we need to prioritize stillness and silence before God. When we simply sit before God in the silence, just as we are, he meets us and begins to change us. Silence can often feel awkward and strangely loud, but the art of silence is something that needs to be practised. God wants to speak to us, guide us and comfort us, but the question is: are we taking time out to listen?

20 JUN

SERVE OTHERS

If only we were kinder,
If only we put others first.
If only we served those in need
and cared enough to quench their thirst.

Let's make a decision to care
and look out for the hurt and the lost,
Let's give our time and attention
and serve others whatever the cost.

21 JUN

Jesus said:

I've loved you the way my Father has loved me. Make yourselves at home in my love. If you keep my commands, you'll remain intimately at home in my love. That's what I've done — kept my Father's commands and made myself at home in his love.

I've told you these things for a purpose: that my joy might be your joy, and your joy wholly mature. This is my command: Love one another the way I loved you. This is the very best way to love. Put your life on the line for your friends. You are my friends when you do the things I command you. I'm no longer calling you servants because servants don't understand what their master is thinking and planning. No, I've named you friends because I've let you in on everything I've heard from the Father.
John 15.9–15, The Message

22 JUN

You are incredible and
irreplaceable.
Don't let anyone ever
tell you otherwise.

23 JUN

FOCUSING ON OUR TRUE SELF

I recently watched a TED talk by Cameron Russell which both challenged and inspired me. The talk was entitled 'Looks aren't everything, believe me, I'm a model', and here's one of the things she said:

> If you're wondering [if you'll be happier if you have thinner thighs and shinier hair, you just need to meet a group of models. They] have the thinnest thighs, the shiniest hair and the coolest clothes, and [yet] they're the most physically insecure people probably on the planet.

When I heard this, I said, 'Excuse me . . . I've been trying so hard to look like a runway model and now you're telling me that even they aren't happy with how they look?!' Nuts, right?

It got me thinking, though. If the people in society who are deemed to be the pinnacle of beauty aren't secure in themselves, then surely this whole confidence, self-assurance thing has to do with something other than 'beauty' itself.

If we look in the Bible, 1 Samuel 16.7 says, 'The LORD does not look at the things people look at. People look at the outward appearance, but the LORD looks at the heart.'

What does it mean to focus on our heart? I'd say this is about focusing on our true self: our strengths, gifts, character and abilities. This quote from US author Anna Quindlen is one of my favourites: 'The thing that is really hard, and really amazing, is giving up on being perfect and beginning the work of becoming yourself.'

Today, as you go about your daily activities, let go of being perfect. Let go of worrying about how you look, and focus on all the other amazing things that make you 'you'.

Jessie

24 JUN

Wherever you go today, there will be opportunities for you to do good. Look out for them.

25 JUN

PATIENTLY WAITING

Waiting for what you are longing for is a bit of a theme in human life. This is because anything worth having is worth waiting for.

Let's say you had arranged to meet a friend on a Saturday to go shopping together. You catch the bus from home but there is so much traffic and so many roadworks that you end up being really late. How long would you want your friend to wait for you? If she waited for only a few minutes before she went home, what would that tell you about how she felt about you? If, however, when you eventually turned up two hours late, you found her sitting on a bench, patiently waiting for you, how would that make you feel?

Waiting is good.

Even though your friend was sitting doing nothing while she waited for you, this nothingness was everything! It was telling you that you are very important to her. It was also telling you that she was the kind of friend worth having: patient, faithful, kind. This experience would strengthen your friendship in a way that no amount of presents and good times together could do.

What about waiting for sex?

Could *not* having sex with your boyfriend actually make your relationship with him deeper?

Could waiting for sex until you get married actually make your marriage stronger?

Could not having sex now, even if you don't know whether you will ever get married, make you more convinced that there is much more to life than sex?

These are big questions, and even if you aren't facing them yet you will one day. Saving sex until marriage doesn't mean it will be mind-blowingly awesome the first time you have it. But it does mean that you will have concentrated on building a relationship based on trust and faithfulness even before you ever have sex. That is the best start to any sexual relationship.

Rachel

26 JUN

I am like an olive tree
    flourishing in the house of God;
I trust in God's unfailing love
    for ever and ever.
For what you have done I will always praise you
    in the presence of your faithful people.
And I will hope in your name,
    for your name is good.

Psalm 52.8–9

27 JUN

BIG DREAMS

One of my favourite Bible verses is found in the Gospel of John, chapter 10, verse 10. Jesus is speaking in this particular verse and he says that although the enemy (also known as Satan or evil) comes to steal, kill and destroy things, he (Jesus) came that we might have life. And not just regular life, either – he actually goes on to describe this life as life to the *full*.

I know that I'm certainly guilty of not always living a hugely 'full' life. I know that I can sometimes find myself playing it small or not dreaming the big dreams God truly wants me to dream. Can you relate? Have you ever found yourself playing down your desires and your dreams for fear of sounding as if you're 'too much' or 'too different'?

Every single dream, desire and plan which is currently in your head and in your heart is not there by accident. It's actually impossible for you to 'out-dream' God when it comes to the plans he has for your life and future. For example, have you ever thought about something in particular which you'd really like to do or be or say and then found yourself too afraid to even *tell* anyone, it's that big? The Bible talks about God being a God of more than we can possibly ask, think or even imagine, which means that it's safe to say that no matter how big your dreams, God has bigger ones for you. So keep dreaming!

Naomi

28 JUN

You are one of a kind!
So beautiful and strong,
Be brave, be yourself and
sing *your* song.

SECURELY CONNECTED

We have this hope as an anchor for the soul, firm and secure.
Hebrews 6.19

The Bible tells us our hope is in Jesus — in the truth that he has won the forgiveness of our sins on the cross, that he has brought us into relationship with God both now and into eternity. When we have this hope, we are held secure. But just like a ship anchored to one position, we are not immune to bobbing. When life is going well we feel calm, but when waves come that rock us it can be hard to hold on to peace.

So often our circumstances take up our focus and attention. We need to view our issues in the light of who he is, his goodness, power and love. We need to train ourselves to look first to our hope, Jesus.

Today you are anchored. You are securely connected to a God who loves you and is for you. Put him at the centre of your horizon today.

Ali

30 JUN

WHAT'S THAT IN MY SUITCASE?

In 2011, I took a trip to Northumberland with my friend Sarah. It was a lonnng way from Essex, but I was really excited about the train journey. What I wasn't so excited about was lugging my case all that way. I had no clue what the weather was going to be like so I packed for rain, sun, snow — you get the idea. It was heavy!

When we finally arrived, I opened my case to unpack and as I moved a T-shirt I saw something that made me jump out of my skin.

A claw.

An actual claw.

I immediately shoved the case away from me to the corner of the room and couldn't go back to it. I was hysterical, but Sarah was laughing. She bravely moved my clothes aside to reveal what was hiding underneath . . . sitting quite comfortably in my case was a massive crab sitting on a stone. Argh! A crab?! It turns out it was this weird dead crab ornament thing that my 'hilarious' brother had hidden in there for a joke.

I sat the crab on my bedside table and thought about how I'd lugged this huge stone all the way up north. My journey would have been so much lighter without it!

If you imagine your life as a suitcase, are there things that you need to get rid of or sort out that are weighing you down? Perhaps it's a name you've been called that you've held on to or a falling out, a painful memory, a failure, a disappointment.

I love these words from Jesus: 'I won't lay anything heavy or ill-fitting on you. Keep company with me and you'll learn to live freely and lightly' (Matthew 11.28, *The Message*).

We can walk around for years with heavy hearts, carrying weights of shame and hurt. Does life feel heavy and as if it's too much to bear? Today, share those things that are painful to carry with Jesus; he cares and wants to lift the weight from your shoulders.

01 JUL

But you'll welcome us with open arms when we run for cover to you.

Psalm 5.11, *The Message*

02 JUL

BIG QUESTIONS: WILL GOD HEAL MY FRIEND? PART 1: ARE MIRACLES POSSIBLE?

A miracle is something that breaks the rules of normal life and can't be explained naturally. It's a situation that has been interrupted by a supernatural power: God.

If I drop a mug, gravity dictates that it will fall to the floor (and probably break, given my track record). If, however, I drop the mug and it stops before it hits the floor without a rational explanation (such as my hand catching it), someone might describe this event as a miracle. Likewise, if a doctor tells a child she'll never walk again but, against scientific prediction, she suddenly can, that could be described as a miracle.

If we believe in a scientific world where things react a certain way, isn't it impossible to believe in miracles? Well, no. It's *because* of science that we can recognize miracles. We know how things should normally react, so when they don't these rare exceptions to the rules appear to be miracles.

When something 'miraculous' happens, people often try to find a natural explanation: it was a trick of the light, adrenaline or coincidence. In some senses, only the person who has experienced the miracle is really able to know whether it was a miracle or not.

Miracles are hard to get our heads around, but if we believe in God it shouldn't be too difficult to also believe in miracles. If God is powerful enough to create the world, why couldn't he perform something out of the ordinary?

In the Gospels, Jesus does many miraculous things: making people better, telling blindness to go away, even raising people from the dead! If these stories are trustworthy (see 3 April for more on this), there's no doubt Jesus *could* heal someone. But do miracles still happen today?

I have seen my fair share of miracles. I've seen people healed from life-threatening illnesses, I've seen hardened criminals' lives completely transformed and I've seen crippling addictions disappear after one prayer. So, if the question was, 'Can God heal my friend?' I think the answer would be a resounding yes. But the real question is, '*Will* he?'

Ruth

BIG QUESTIONS: WILL GOD HEAL MY FRIEND? PART 2: WHY DOESN'T EVERYONE GET HEALED?

I will remember 12 December 2012 for ever: the day my mum was told that her cancer had completely disappeared. However, on that same day my best friend's mum tragically lost her battle with cancer.

People sometimes describe this as the 'now and not yet' of God's kingdom. God came into the world, in human form, as Jesus. After dying and miraculously rising again, Jesus left us his Holy Spirit, meaning God is with us *now*. Miracles are possible *now*. However, there is still a 'not yet' element. Heartbreakingly, some people don't get better.

When prayers are answered, we see glimpses of heaven on earth and a foretaste of what life will be like in the future. But when this doesn't happen, it's confusing, upsetting and disappointing. It's hard to know why some prayers aren't answered, but it absolutely doesn't mean God cares more about the people who *are* healed. Neither does it mean he doesn't listen, nor that we don't matter.

It's horribly painful when we don't get the answers we want, but I don't think this should put us off praying. Praying draws us closer to the only Person who knows what we're going through, who can breathe peace into our tragedy and promises a future where every tear will be wiped away.

When a friend of mine died, I was furious with God for ignoring my prayers. A few days later, someone in church read Isaiah 49.14–16: 'Jerusalem says, "The Lord has deserted us; the LORD has forgotten us"' (*New Living Translation*).

The passage goes on:

> Never! Can a mother forget her nursing child?
> Can she feel no love for the child she has borne?
> But even if that were possible,
> I would not forget you!
> See, I have written your name on the palms of my hands.
> Always in my mind is a picture of Jerusalem's walls in ruins.

We may not always get the answers we desperately want, but we can be sure that God has not forgotten us, that he joins us in the ruins and holds us in our pain.

Ruth

04 JUL

No act of kindness,
no matter how small,
is ever wasted.

05 JUL

GOD IS NOT DISTANT

> God above you,
> God below you,
> God beside you,
> God before you,
> God behind you.

I used to have this written on a little piece of card stuck underneath a shelf above my bed. It meant that when I lay down to sleep and looked up I could read it, and when I woke up in the morning it would be the first thing I'd see. I used to read it and be reminded of the fact that, no matter what happened that day, God was and is so very close.

God is not distant; he walks beside you every day of your life and longs for you to acknowledge his presence and walk with him. So, wherever you go today, whatever happens, you can be absolutely certain of one thing — God is right there with you.

06 JUL

Jesus said, 'Everyone who drinks this water will get thirsty again and again. Anyone who drinks the water I give will never thirst — not ever. The water I give will be an artesian spring within, gushing fountains of endless life.'

John 4.13–14, *The Message*

07 JUL

HOPE-FILLED PEOPLE

Those who have the most hope will always have the most influence. Let hope be the characteristic you're known for.
Bill Johnson, US pastor

I heard this phrase while attending a conference and it really stuck with me. I think sometimes we decide that either we're born with hope or we're not, the way you're either born with freckles or you're born without them. But hope isn't like this. Hope is something that lies deep within each one of us and over time we can help it develop and grow.

I think one of the main ways we can grow hope in our lives is by monitoring the thoughts racing round in our heads. Have you ever found yourself thinking, 'It's always going to be like this,' or 'Everyone's always going to hate me,' or 'Life is never going to get any better'? I have! But when we're confronted with thoughts like this, we need to take a moment to ask ourselves whether that's true or whether we are believing lies about ourselves which are preventing us from chasing our dreams and discovering our potential.

Hope is infectious. It's contagious, and it draws people to you: by having hope you're refusing to believe that just because something is one way it'll always be that way. It's the ability to believe that the end result is not determined yet; we can make a difference and change things. Hope-filled people are people who dare to believe that things could be different – and not just different, but better.

Hope-filled people are people who say, 'Yes I *can* do this, I'm going to step out and take a risk.'

How can you bring more hope into your day today?

Rachel

God did it for us. Out of sheer generosity he put us in right standing with himself. A pure gift. He got us out of the mess we're in and restored us to where he always wanted us to be. And he did it by means of Jesus Christ.

Romans 3.23–24, *The Message*

09 JUL

SCARS

We all have scars, don't we?

Whether they be the marks of that failed football tackle, an accident with the hair straighteners, a battle with self-harm or even an operation, everyone has scars.

Scars are nothing to be ashamed of; they are a sign of the things we've been through, the stories we carry. There are many practical ways you can find to deal with scarring, but the most important thing is to come to terms with where you've journeyed in your life.

I have a lot of self-harm scars. For many years I thought they made me ugly, but the truth was they were just a map of the roads I'd gone down trying to find peace.

I didn't find peace in my scars, but in the scars of someone else.

When Jesus was resurrected, he still had the scars that had been caused by his crucifixion — but they became the sign that he had risen from the dead!

Scars needn't be a source of shame, because they show the paths we've been down. If we let them, they can remind us what Jesus has done for us and that we're loved by God.

Rachael

10 JUL

PRACTISE BEING BRAVE

I'm a bit of a worrier. I worried all through school; I worried about my exams, about whether I would get into college and then about what I would do after college. I thought by now it would have changed but it hasn't — the last time I spoke on stage I got myself so worried that I ended up being very sick afterwards. Not cool. Looking back I totally missed the fun of that event because I was so focused on my fear.

When I look through my diary and see some of the things I have to do this year, I shudder with nerves and worry. There have been so many days that I've just wanted to hide away because I've been worried about facing the camera or the people. But by being constantly worried about what's next, I'm actually missing the enjoyment of the now.

I've spent far too much of my time being worried and doubting my abilities, and things have to change. Funnily enough, as I typed up this entry I accidentally wrote 'warrior' instead of 'worrier'. So I've decided I want to be a warrior rather than a worrier — I want to be brave and conquer this constant need to worry. It's not healthy and it certainly doesn't make me happy. I want to face my fears one day at a time rather than looking ahead, worried about what may or may not happen.

Are you a worrier? If so, join me in becoming a warrior, practising being brave and trying to conquer your worries. Don't waste your time any longer worrying about what may or may not happen tomorrow, but instead make the most of your time by enjoying today.

11 JUL

If your first concern is to look after yourself, you'll never find yourself. But if you forget about yourself and look to me, you'll find both yourself and me.

Matthew 10.39, *The Message*

CHANGE THE SOUNDTRACK

When you watch a film, your eyes see images that tell a story. But it's often not the images but the soundtrack that is responsible for the way you *feel*. The music can make you feel tense, nervous, happy, excited, relieved . . . all kinds of responses to music you don't even realize you're hearing!

When you think of God, when you pray, when you read your Bible – what do you hear and what do you feel? Often without realizing it, we tune in to a different message from the one God is speaking. Though the words may say something wonderful, we feel that God is cross, that he is not good, that we are not loved and we don't make the grade.

God wants to change this soundtrack. He wants us to hear how good he is, how much he loves and forgives us. Let's ask God to show us where we are listening to the wrong tune, and ask him to help us to hold on to the wonderful truths that the Bible teaches about who he is and who we are in him.

Ali

13 JUL

If you see something beautiful
in someone, speak it!

Ruthie Lindsey, author and speaker

14 JUL

OPEN UP

Sometimes we get into a habit of keeping ourselves to ourselves and are closed off from the world in front of us. So often we live internally and don't make an effort to interact with the people around us. What we all need to remember is that there is so much that we can learn from one another. It's in sharing a smile, a 'Hello' or a 'How are you?' that we can encourage the people we come into contact with. Yes, I know it can feel silly or nerve-wracking saying 'Good morning' to someone you don't know, but the more you speak with new people, the easier it gets.

So I want to challenge you to take a brave step and speak to people that you're not familiar with: the person who serves you, your bus driver, the shop assistant or that girl at school who looks alone. Together let's take a step towards opening up and living outwardly.

There is a story behind every person,
a reason why they are the way they
are. Don't be quick to judge. Be kind
and assume the best.

Nicky Gumbel, developer of the Alpha Course
and vicar of Holy Trinity Brompton

16 JUL

WONDER WOMEN: PART 1

When I read the Bible, I am so inspired by the wonderful women who have bravely and faithfully followed God. I love reading the accounts of these real, strong women who have overcome challenge and fulfilled their potential. Over the next few days, we're going to be looking at their stories . . .

The bleeding woman (Mark 5.25–34)

There was a woman who was in a really bad place. She had been bleeding for 12 years and no one could heal her. She'd spent all she had on doctors and was desperate to be free from her condition. I love the story in the Gospel of Mark where we read about her immense bravery.

> *When she heard about Jesus, she came up behind him in the crowd and touched his cloak, because she thought, 'If I just touch his clothes, I will be healed.' Immediately her bleeding stopped and she felt in her body that she was freed from her suffering.*
> Mark 5.27–29

When Jesus asks, 'Who touched me?' she falls at his feet and, trembling with fear, tells him the whole truth. Jesus replies to her, 'Daughter, your faith has healed you. Go in peace and be freed from your suffering' (Mark 5.34).

As she stepped into that crowd, she would have known so well that if she was noticed she would be in big trouble. Her bleeding made her unclean, a complete outcast from society — nobody would want to be anywhere near her. Yet she courageously steps into that crowd because she's desperate for Jesus. Her faith in Jesus is beautiful and inspiring! It's such an incredible moment where the Son of God speaks directly to her, heals her suffering and tells her she can now live in peace. Wow! This woman reminds us to stay close to Jesus, to desire him and to have great faith in his power. But she also teaches us that incredible things can happen when we take that first brave step!

Do you need healing? Do you need peace? Have the faith to reach out to Jesus today and experience his great love and power.

17 JUL

WONDER WOMEN: PART 2

The woman at the well (John 4.1–42)
Have you heard the story about the woman who met Jesus at a well? They
were in a town called Sychar in Samaria, and it was the middle of the day when
Jesus asked the woman to give him a drink. It would have been shocking to
everyone around that Jesus would speak to her, since she was a Samaritan and
Jesus was a Jew (they didn't mix!).

> *She said to Jesus, 'You are a Jew, and I am a Samaritan woman. Why are you
> asking me for a drink?'*
>
> *Jesus replied, 'If you only knew the gift God has for you and who you are
> speaking to, you would ask me, and I would give you living water.'*
> John 4.9–10, *New Living Translation*

There's this incredible moment where Jesus goes on to tell her that he knows
all about her and the fact that she has multiple husbands. She's shocked that he
knows her secret, and as she stands there, amazed that he knows all about her,
he declares that he is the Messiah, the one they've all been waiting for.

This woman races back to town so fast that she leaves her water pot behind!
She tells anyone who will listen about Jesus and 'Many of the Samaritans . . .
believed in him because of the woman's testimony' (v. 39).

I absolutely love this story. It reminds us that, despite our failures, Jesus wants
to speak to us and use us to spread his life-giving message. I love the way he
tells the woman that he knows all about her, and she's blown away by it. This
happened over 2,000 years ago, but today Jesus is still offering you life-giving
water so that you'll never be thirsty again. Remember today, if you get it wrong,
don't run and hide from God. He's still close and he still cares for you — and
even more than that, he can use you as a light to others.

If you ache, sink down into his life-giving water and let him soothe you.

If you're feeling dirty, allow God to cleanse you.

If you're thirsty, ask God to quench that thirst today.

WONDER WOMEN: PART 3

Mary, the mother of Jesus (Luke 1.26–38)

Mary is perhaps the most famous woman in the Bible. When she was around 14 years old, she was visited by an angel who told her she had favour with God and would conceive a baby, who would be the Son of God. (Can you *imagine* the shock?!) The Bible says she was afraid and questions how it could be since she was a virgin. But by the end of the angel's visit she declares, 'I am the Lord's servant. May everything you have said about me come true' (Luke 1.38, *New Living Translation*). What an amazing statement of faith! She's declaring that she will serve God and bring this new life into the world.

If you're young and thinking that your life will really get going once you're older, or that you'll only find your purpose once you're in your 20s or 30s, remember: Mary was thought to be around the age of 14 when the angel visited her! That's when she declared that she would serve God and join in with what he was doing in the world. Mary really teaches us to trust God and believe that he can use us to bring love and freedom to our communities, friendships and families.

The brilliant news is that God is still at work in our world today, and he brought you here for this moment in history for a reason. Could *this* be the day when you speak the same words as Mary: 'I am the Lord's servant'?

19 JUL

WONDER WOMEN: PART 4

Ruth (the book of Ruth)

There was a lady called Naomi whose husband and two sons had died. She told her two daughters-in-law, Ruth and Orpah, to go and start a new life elsewhere. Orpah leaves to go back to her people and find another husband, but Ruth shows the most beautiful faithfulness as she says these words: 'Don't urge me to leave you or turn back from you. Where you go I will go, and where you stay I will stay. Your people will be my people and your God my God' (Ruth 1.16).

I love the way Ruth doesn't abandon Naomi but promises to always be her family and never leave her. It's an amazing example for us of what it means to faithfully stick by someone and put that person before ourselves.

Ruth's life story doesn't read easily; it's dramatic and it's sad. She spent ten years being looked down on because she couldn't have children, and then her husband died. Eventually, after moving to a new place, we see her meet a kind man called Boaz, but still the journey of their relationship is a challenging one. The problem is, another man has been lined up to marry Ruth, according to Hebrew custom!

I'm pleased to say that the story has a brilliant end where Boaz and Ruth finally get married and God blesses them with a son. And do you know the really exciting thing? This baby was called Obed, who was the father of Jesse. Jesse was the father of King David, and generations later their descendant Joseph was born, who married Mary, the mother of Jesus! Ruth would have never known how incredible her family line would become! Like Ruth, we will meet obstacles in our life that we have to navigate.

All of us experience successes and failures, but Ruth's story reminds us to hold on when the going gets tough and to trust in God's perfect plan.

If life isn't going well at the moment, be encouraged that you're not at the end of the story yet.

20 JUL

May the God of hope fill you with all joy and peace as you trust in him, so that you may overflow with hope by the power of the Holy Spirit.

Romans 15.13

21 JUL

GRACE CHANGES EVERYTHING

Nobody likes talking about sin. It makes us feel rubbish and guilty, as though we're not good enough. But I love talking about it!

I love it because, actually, sin is all about grace and I know how much I need God's grace. Left to myself, I'm selfishly ambitious, arrogant and hard towards the people I love. My hunger for happiness (or simply to feel all right) can sometimes drive me to selfishness where I only care about myself. I know how deep my need for cleaning goes — and I also know that by myself I can only clean up the surface (a bit). Only God can clean the sickness of sin that lives inside me.

The reason why God hates sin in our lives is because it is a bit like a 'keep-God-out' sign that holds us prisoners to our insecurity and selfishness, and ensures we remain broken. Sin is a strong and cruel slave-master. Have you noticed in your own life that you find yourself returning time and again to the sin you commit as a way of feeling better about the sin you commit? It's a damaging cycle that needs to be broken. No matter how strong we are, on our own we can't break it. We need a Saviour for that. The Apostle Paul knew this better than anyone. After years of murdering Christians, he was met by Jesus in a powerful and blinding vision. He got to see the depth of his darkness as well as the even bigger embrace of grace.

No sin is too big for God; his grace is sufficient for you. Spend time with God today, saying sorry for the things that have kept him apart from you, and ask him to fill you afresh with his love and grace.

Rachel

22 JUL

We have this hope as an anchor for the soul, firm and secure.

Hebrews 6.19

"

I'm happy from the inside out,
    and from the outside in, I'm firmly formed.
You canceled my ticket to hell —
    that's not my destination!

Now you've got my feet on the life path,
    all radiant from the shining of your face.
Ever since you took my hand,
    I'm on the right way.

Psalm 16.9–11, *The Message*

"

RELATIONSHIP WITH JESUS

The Bible often talks about a group of religious leaders called the Pharisees. They were strict teachers of religious law, and they didn't like Jesus very much because he often did things *very* differently from them. They thought this was awful because they believed they were doing everything right and living a life which everyone else should be following. The problem? They'd missed the point. They'd got so bogged down in religious teaching and law that they'd completely forgotten the fact that God desired a *relationship* with them.

A relationship with God isn't about following a set of rules. In a lot of ways, it's the same as a relationship with our friends or family — he wants us to simply spend time with him, to tell him about our greatest joys, our foremost worries, our deepest struggles. We can't earn his love by doing good things or attending every event put on by our church. His love for us is not dependent on what we've done or what we haven't done. Romans 5.8 tells us this: 'But God demonstrates his own love for us in this: while we were still sinners, Christ died for us.'

Spend time with Jesus today — he's looking for a relationship with you!

Naomi

25JUL

As your limbs lengthen, as your hair grows longer and your body changes shape, as hormones race through your body waking you up to womanhood, may you know that Jesus is working in you his great and perfect plan. May you begin to look more and more like him so that your life brings hope and blessing to the world.

Rachel

26JUL

Thank you for this day right here,
Thank you that I've got nothing to fear,
Thank you for my friends and family,
And I thank you God for loving me.

27 JUL

MAKE THE MOST OF YOUR TIME

Is your phone having a positive or negative effect on your life? I only ask because I don't think mine is doing me much good.

Every spare second of the day I'm on it, checking my social media, online shopping, catching up on the latest celebrity gossip, scrolling endlessly through YouTube – I can waste hours and hours.

Last night I spent an hour and ten minutes scrolling through the sale section of my favourite shop and never bought a thing. Now, it's not wrong of me to do that, but when I put my phone down I thought, 'I just wasted 70 minutes of my life doing nothing.'

There are so many other things that I could have done in those 70 minutes that would have been a better use of my time, I've got books to read, I could have practised the piano, I've got rooms to tidy, I could have written to my god-daughter or called my friend who I haven't spoken to in months. Instead, I'm horrendously addicted to this screen in my hand; it screams for my attention because there's always a new video or image to see. The reality is that it's eating away at my day and ultimately my life. (It sounds dramatic, but it's true!)

So if you're anything like me and recognize that your phone addiction needs a bit of attention, here's what we've decided in our house. We're going to start to tackle this by having one evening a week phone-free.

It felt really weird the first night: you wonder what you're missing out on, you keep going to pick up your phone from beside you and then you realize it's not there! But do you know what? It's actually really refreshing! It makes you realize just how much attention you give it. So why don't you join us? Start by having just one evening a week tech-free and make the most of your time.

28 JUL

And surely I am with you always,
to the very end of the age.

Matthew 28.20

29 JUL

Leave me alone with God as much as may be.
As the tide draws the waters close in upon the shore,
make me an island, set apart,
alone with you, God, holy to you.

Then, with the turning of the tide,
prepare me to carry your presence to the busy world beyond,
the world that rushes in on me till the waters come again
and fold me back to you.

St Aidan of Lindisfarne

30 JUL

Be who God
meant you to be
and you will set the
world on fire.

St Catherine of Siena

31 JUL

AUGUST

BE YOUR FRIEND

Recently, I was getting ready to meet some friends for a catch-up, and as I passed the mirror in our hall I heard myself say, 'Urgh, you look a state!' I talk to myself quite a lot but that day I realized how many of my comments were negative about myself — it really stuck out to me.

I heard someone say, a while ago, that we should try to talk to ourselves the way we would to a friend, someone we are close to and love. I certainly don't do that — if I spoke to my friends the way I speak to myself I'd have no friends left!

There's power in your words to build up or tear down. If you're starting to realize that, like me, you've been tearing yourself down with your thoughts and words, let's start to change that and become a friend of ourselves!

Why don't you choose one of the following statements and keep it at the forefront of your mind today? Say it out loud as often as you can, think about it and keep an eye out for the way you talk to yourself today.

I am strong.
I am lovely.
I am not alone.
I am lovable.
I am enough.
I am beautiful.
I am brave.

01 AUG

Jesus said: 'I have come that they may have life, and have it to the full.'
John 10.10

HOW GENEROUS ARE YOU?

The word 'generosity' often makes people think of giving money, but I don't just mean money. I mean: are you generous with your time, your things, your words and your attention?

The opposite of living a life of generosity would be to live selfishly and that's a lonely way to live. I read an article recently that said this:

> Year after year, more and more studies are highlighting the benefits of generosity on both our physical and mental health. Not only does generosity reduce stress, support one's physical health, enhance one's sense of purpose and naturally fight depression, it is also shown to increase one's lifespan.
> Lisa Firestone, 'The benefits of generosity', huffingtonpost.com

How great is that? Generosity is actually in our best interests!

But, you know, being a generous person isn't something that just happens by chance; we've actually got to make a conscious decision to become generous as we live our lives. So can you make that decision today? How will you be generous to the people you meet today?

03 AUG

COME BACK TO THE TRUTH

Ephesians 2.10 is my absolute favourite Bible verse! It says this in the *New Living Translation*: 'For we are God's masterpiece. He has created us anew in Christ Jesus, so we can do the good things he planned for us long ago.'

There's so much truth in this quote! For starters, we're God's. Everything that we are is a gift from him. We're his masterpiece. A masterpiece is a masterpiece because there is nothing else in the world like it. It also means we're of outstanding craftsmanship. When you doubt yourself, come back to that truth. You're worth so much that God created good plans, especially for you, before the beginning of time.

Thank you, God, that you care for us so deeply. Help me to live in that truth today.

Jessie

04 AUG

So, friends, confirm God's invitation to you, his choice of you. Don't put it off; do it now. Do this, and you'll have your life on a firm footing, the streets paved and the way wide open into the eternal kingdom of our Master and Savior, Jesus Christ.

2 Peter 1.10–11, *The Message*

05 AUG

GOAL-SETTING AND PLAN-PREPPING

'Fail to prepare, prepare to fail.' I heard this a lot growing up, especially in my teenage years as I worked hard to do the best I could at school and beyond. I was continually told that the key to success was in the preparation, and even though I'm sure I used to roll my eyes a bit upon hearing this back then, now I couldn't agree more!

Whenever I set myself clear intentions and goals regarding a particular project, I'm a lot more able to follow through on my plans — not only because I'm holding myself accountable, but also because I've told people that these are my plans. This isn't all, though, of course. There's a sense of achievement in crossing things off a 'to do' list, isn't there?

So what goals do *you* have? What are the things *you*'ve always said you'd do and yet found yourself constantly saying 'tomorrow' instead? Today could be the day you decide that you're no longer going to put them off! A way I've found especially helpful in setting goals is to write them down, and in fact this type of method is actually pretty biblical. There's a passage in Habakkuk where God says to 'write down the revelation [or vision] and make it plain' (2.2). And so, today, grab a notebook or a journal and start writing down your vision and setting out your goals, and then make it happen!

Naomi

06 AUG

EVERY DAY WE NEED TO SAY YES

Whoever wants to be my disciple must deny themselves and take up their cross daily and follow me. For whoever wants to save their life will lose it, but whoever loses their life for me will save it. What good is it for someone to gain the whole world, and yet lose or forfeit their very self?
Luke 9.23–25

Following Jesus is not about becoming a better person, it's about becoming a new person. But our transformation doesn't stop at the point where we say yes to Jesus. In fact, it starts there. Every day we need to say yes to the new creation God is shaping us into. That's what it means to yield yourself to God. It's the daily and deliberate handing over of your will to God. And it can hurt sometimes, because we're rebels by inclination.

Can you see what God wants you to do with your life?

Surrender it.

Rachel

07 AUG

What is the price of two sparrows — one copper coin? But not a single sparrow can fall to the ground without your Father knowing it. And the very hairs on your head are all numbered. So don't be afraid; you are more valuable to God than a whole flock of sparrows.

Matthew 10.29–31, *New Living Translation*

08 AUG

WE ALL NEED SUPPORT

With anthems of independent women and 'girl power', it can be pretty easy to think it might be a sign of weakness to ask for help or share the fact that you want or even need some support. But the truth is, you need it. Not just you but me as well. In fact, we all need support from time to time.

A listening ear, a friendly face, a shoulder to cry on — all these things are priceless and each one of them is totally essential from time to time as we live life alongside one another. We were never meant to do this alone. We were never meant to struggle and stress about all the things which come our way totally independent of anyone else. When God first created humankind, he actually said it was 'not good' for man to be alone and so he created Eve.

It's not weakness to share the fact that you'd like some support in a particular area. In fact, it can be a huge sign of strength and a rejection of pride. If you do feel a little alone and as though you don't have anyone to turn to at this moment, be assured that God is *always* with you and promises he'll never leave you. Run to him today — he's waiting for you!

Naomi

09 AUG

BIG QUESTIONS: WHY DOES GOD LET NATURAL DISASTERS HAPPEN?

The Bible says that God created a perfect world but humans decided to go their own way, which resulted in disaster. Human rebellion didn't just affect human relationships; it created a brokenness in the whole universe.

Our planet needs events like hurricanes, earthquakes and flooding to function. Hurricanes bring rain to drought-prone areas and help balance the air temperature. Flooding brings nutrients to the soil and volcanic ash releases minerals. Without these, plant and food growth would be very difficult. Likewise, tectonic plate movement (which can lead to earthquakes) helps move nutrients around under the earth's crust, while volcanoes help release pressure and excess gas. Without tectonic activity, we would have limited safe water and there would be no mountains, continents or islands.

The earth is more stable and experiences fewer natural disasters than other planets. For instance, Venus contains numerous active volcanoes and Neptune recently experienced an extreme storm the size of the earth! Life as we know it would be impossible on any other planet.

Sadly, much of the damage caused by natural disasters is due to humans living in unstable areas. Many people who live in these areas are the poorest in society, who cannot afford accommodation elsewhere so end up living by fault lines, in storm-prone areas or on dangerous coasts. For example, an earthquake in wealthy California killed 57 people in 1989, whereas an earthquake of a smiliar size in impoverished Haiti killed 230,000 in 2010.

Poverty and inequality are the result of poor human choices, and these can affect vulnerable people who often have no influence. When God created us, he gave us freedom to make our own decisions, which tragically can lead to disastrous consequences. The Bible says that God has offered us a way out of the pain we've caused: 'God put the world square with himself through the Messiah, giving the world a fresh start by offering forgiveness of sins' (2 Corinthians 5.19, *The Message*). And while God invites us to work with him to bring an end to suffering now, it's only when Jesus returns that we'll see complete restoration. One day, there will be no more tregedy and death (Revelation 21.4).

Ruth

10 AUG

Whatever is true, whatever is noble, whatever is right, whatever is pure, whatever is lovely, whatever is admirable — if anything is excellent or praiseworthy — think about such things.

Philippians 4.8

11 AUG

Peter said, 'Change your life. Turn to God and be baptized, each of you, in the name of Jesus Christ, so your sins are forgiven. Receive the gift of the Holy Spirit. The promise is targeted to you and your children, but also to all who are far away — whomever, in fact, our Master God invites.'

Acts 2.38–39, *The Message*

12 AUG

BIG QUESTIONS: IF GOD FORGIVES EVERYTHING, DOES IT MATTER WHAT I DO?

'Sin' literally means 'to miss the mark'. Sin isn't just murder, theft or drug-dealing, it's anything that misses the bullseye of God's perfect standard.

When we do something bad, there are consequences (especially if we're caught!). But the message of Christianity is that God has forgiven our sin, taking the punishment and consequences on himself so that we can be free. To be forgiven, all we have to do is say sorry or 'repent', which translated from the Greek means 'to change your mind' or 'do an about-turn'. If you ask for forgiveness and repent, you actively turn away from sin.

When people experience God's forgiveness, it often results in a life change. This is true of characters in the Bible, and there are also lots of modern-day examples (see iamsecond.com).

Romans 6.1–2 (*The Message*) says:

> *So what do we do? Keep on sinning so God can keep on forgiving? I should hope not! If we've left the country where sin is sovereign, how can we still live in our old house there? Or didn't you realize we packed up and left there for good?*

Through God's forgiveness we are given a new life. We will still miss the mark, but God's forgiveness isn't just a once-and-for-all thing.

Because God forgives everything, we could, in theory, do whatever we want. However, in order to ask for forgiveness, we need to actually be sorry. If we keep deliberately sinning, we're probably not sorry and don't actually *want* to be forgiven!

If we're in a relationship with God, we won't want to keep sinning. Think of a parent or carer you have a good relationship with. If he or she asked you not to do certain things, you'd probably try to avoid these so you didn't hurt that person's feelings and put a barrier between you. You wouldn't intentionally act in a way that distances your parent or carer from you. It's the same with God. Nothing we do can make him love us more (or less), but as we draw close to him we will want to live in a way that pleases him.

Ruth

13 AUG

PRACTICE MAKES PERFECT

We've all got our quirky, weird and wondrous ways; let's accept ourselves as we are.

All right, I know this is easier said than done, but we all know the saying, *'Practice makes perfect'*.

So today practise being perfectly you, nothing more, nothing less.

14 AUG

For the LORD your God is living among you.
    He is a mighty savior.
He will take delight in you with gladness.
    With his love, he will calm all your fears.
    He will rejoice over you with joyful songs.

Zephaniah 3.17, *New Living Translation*

15 AUG

SHOULDER TO SHOULDER

Jesus is this incredible ancient historical figure who was walking around in the Middle East over 2,000 years ago. He probably had a beard, dark hair and dark skin. He very quickly had celebrity status, not because he made everything centre around himself but because he claimed that he himself was God, and that the way to know God and to know life in all its fullness was to live as he lived.

Jesus said the way to really know yourself is to forget about yourself, forget about trying to make yourself perfect, forget about trying to control what everyone else thinks about you, forget about trying to be clever and successful — that's not the path to happiness. The path to happiness is to know God and to live your life by God's instructions. Jesus was incredibly radical, and actually he was murdered for it.

Jesus is everything to me, and I want my life to be all about him. To me, he is very real and very close, and the older I get the more I sense his presence in good times and in bad times. I used to only experience his presence at particular high points or particular low points in my life, when I felt I needed him. But the older I get the more I experience his friendship, him next to me shoulder to shoulder. I believe that he has incredible power and authority to do the most important things in my life that need changing.

I believe that his life, his death and his resurrection completely released me from the curse of death. Even though I still feel fear and uncertainty about the future, I am increasingly confident that he is able to draw me through everything and ultimately take me through death to the other side, where I'll be living for ever in his presence.

The more I get to know Jesus, the more I really want to get to know him.

Rachel

Watch the way you talk. Let nothing foul or dirty come out of your mouth. Say only what helps, each word a gift.

Ephesians 4.29, *The Message*

17 AUG

Stop.
Breathe.
Take a moment to pause.
And in that moment open your heart,
to God who's loved you from the start.
Take a moment to recognize him there,
Acknowledge his presence, his peace, his care.

Too often we go about our day,
Ignoring him as we go on our way,
But stop.
Breathe.
Take a moment to pause today.
For if you listen carefully,
He's calling out your name.

AS YOU SPEAK TODAY

I love words; as a writer I enjoy playing around with them, and writing is the way I come to terms with things and make sense of the world. We have to take care of our words, whether they're spoken or written, because they can have a great deal of power. It's our choice whether we use words to encourage or discourage, to offer comfort or conflict.

As you speak today, consider what the effect might be. Proverbs 15.4 says that 'gentle words bring life and health'. It doesn't mean that we don't say difficult things when we need to, but that we do it in order to encourage and challenge.

How can you be gentle with your words today?

Rachael

19 AUG

Live in peace with each other.

1 Thessalonians 5.13

20 AUG

FRIENDSHIP TAKES WORK

My friend Nicci has a little sign in her lounge that says, 'A friend is one of the nicest things you can have and one of the loveliest things you can be.'

Friendships are nice and lovely, but do you know what? They take work! So here are a few things to remember to keep our friendships healthy . . .

- *Don't gossip:* don't bad mouth one another; don't talk negatively about your friends behind their backs. It destroys friendship. Also, if someone shares something with you that you know you should keep to yourself, keep it to yourself.
- *Be honest:* don't pretend to be something you're not in your friendships, and also remember to be truthful with your words.
- *Say sorry:* if you know that you've got something wrong, don't be too proud to say sorry. It's not an easy word to say and it doesn't always sort everything out, but it's a start.
- *Forgive:* we've all done things wrong, things that have upset one another. Forgiveness is really tough but it's important.
- *Listen:* listening is a really important part of a friendship. Don't let someone's words wash over you, in one ear and out of the other. Take time to really hear what your friend is saying.
- *Support:* be there for your friends, make sure they know that you've got their back and are available for them, even when it might be inconvenient to you.
- *Be reliable:* if you say to your friend that you'll do something for him or her, do it. Or if you've said that you'll be somewhere at a certain time, then be there! Keep the commitments you make and be trustworthy. It's really important to be able to trust a friend.

These are things we *all* need to get better at, but don't let this list overwhelm you! Slowly but surely we'll get there if we try. The best thing to remember is that if you want a good friend, then be a good friend.

Above all else, guard your heart, for everything you do flows from it.

Proverbs 4.23

22 AUG

A NEW START

I used to swear in the playground at school. I knew I shouldn't be doing it, but everyone else was and I really wanted to fit in. However, the day I was baptized, at the age of 15, I read this verse: 'Anyone who belongs to Christ has become a new person. The old life is gone; a new life has begun!' (2 Corinthians 5.17, *New Living Translation*).

The words I said in the playground at school were something I wanted to change about myself, and I felt as if my baptism was a fresh new start!

Only, the day after my baptism, I stood in the playground and that word that I hated just popped out. I felt gutted. And then in the evening I had an argument with my parents. I sat on my bed, sobbing that I'd ruined my 'new start'. I didn't feel like a new person, I was just the old, moody Meg, saying and doing things that I shouldn't.

If only someone had let me in on the reality of being a Christian: we're going to get it wrong, but God *still* loves us! Even in our messiest moments and on our darkest days, when we feel unlovely and unlovable, our Father is there with open arms, welcoming us back. The brilliant news is that there's nothing you can do to make God love you any more or any less: he covers us with his grace. Grace is God's love, blessing and kindness being offered to us even though we don't deserve it . . . and I definitely don't deserve it!

I still have moody days and I still say things I shouldn't, but that doesn't take away this new life that God has given me. On the cross, Jesus took on all the things we'll ever do wrong. He died with those sins and took them to the grave. When we accept that sacrifice, and make a decision to give our lives to God, we are promised a new and eternal life — that's a gift for ever!

Have you accepted the beautiful sacrifice Jesus made for you? Grab it with both hands! Thank him with all your heart! Each day is a new start with God.

23 AUG

BIG QUESTIONS: DOES SCIENCE DISPROVE GOD?

So many people think God and science are opposite ways of looking at life. Either the earth popped into existence through some sort of godly magic or it emerged through scientific processes. But what if they're just different ways of looking at life?

If I boil a kettle, science can explain the process (electric current heats the element, which heats the water) but it cannot tell me why the kettle boiled (I wanted a cup of tea!).

Science deals with questions of how but it doesn't answer questions of purpose, origin or even things like love. Science can't tell me why I'm here, what the point of life is or what sort of person I should become.

Science and God answer different questions, but that doesn't mean they cancel each other out. Take my smartphone as an example. Ask me how it came into existence and I could give you two very different answers.

I could talk you through the component parts and tell you about the 'dual ion exchange process at a molecular level'. Or I could simply say: 'Steve Jobs'. The man behind my smartphone. Both are equally valid answers (though one is much easier to remember!). Likewise, when talking about the existence of our universe, we don't need to pick either a scientific explanation or God as Creator; the two can fit together.

Christians believe that God created the world and has left us clues as to why we're here and what he thinks of us, but it is science that shows us how the world formed and how it works.

Science doesn't contradict God. In fact, lots of world-class scientists think science points people right to God. Louis Pasteur, who created pasteurization and was the founder of immunization (without him we wouldn't have injections or tasty cheese), said: 'The more I study nature, the more I stand amazed at the work of the creator. Science brings men nearer to God.' And Albert Einstein, the award-winning physicist with the big hair, said: 'The more I study science, the more I believe in God.'

Ruth

24 AUG

The LORD is my strength and my shield; my heart trusts in him, and he helps me.

Psalm 28.7

25 AUG

THROW OPEN YOUR PAGES

In the front of my Bible, I've written the words 'You are the God who sees me, the God who knows me, the God who hears me.' Every time I read it I'm reminded that God knows me better than I know myself, that he hears me when I speak to him and that he sees and understands the situation I'm facing. He's right there so very close beside me.

Yes, it's great and encouraging, *but* it's also a challenge because it reminds me that he hears the words that I say and he sees where I go and what I do each day. Nothing is hidden from him — my good and my bad, he sees it all. It's all out in the open.

There's a great psalm in the Bible that says this:

> *Investigate my life, O God,*
> *find out everything about me;*
> *Cross-examine and test me,*
> *get a clear picture of what I'm about;*
> *See for yourself whether I've done anything wrong —*
> *then guide me on the road to eternal life.*
> Psalm 139.23–24, *The Message*

I just love those words! They're inviting God into all that you are and all that you do, asking him to guide you on the right path. It's a bold prayer, not one to be taken lightly, but how incredible to have the God of the universe testing and leading you in life! Earlier on in that psalm it says, 'Search me like an open book.' Is the book of your life closed off to him? Today, throw open your pages to him and let him in; he wants the best for you.

26 AUG

Father,
I abandon myself into your hands;
do with me what you will.
Whatever you may do, I thank you:
I am ready for all, I accept all.

Let only your will be done in me,
and in all your creatures —
I wish no more than this, O Lord.

Into your hands I commend my soul:
I offer it to you with all the love of my heart,
for I love you, Lord, and so need to give myself,
to surrender myself into your hands without reserve,
and with boundless confidence,
for you are my Father.

Charles de Foucauld, French Catholic martyr

27 AUG

Run the race set
out for you.

28 AUG

I waited and waited and waited for GOD.
    At last he looked; finally he listened.
He lifted me out of the ditch,
    pulled me from deep mud.
He stood me up on a solid rock
    to make sure I wouldn't slip.
He taught me how to sing the latest God-song,
    a praise-song to our God.
More and more people are seeing this:
    they enter the mystery,
    abandoning themselves to GOD.

Psalm 40.1–3, *The Message*

29 AUG

ACCESS ALL AREAS

One day I had a huge row with my mum. It wasn't the first, wouldn't be the last, but it was a defining moment because at the end of the row I told her she was never to mention that particular issue to me again. It was out of bounds, off the table, an absolute no-go area between her and me.

Years later I did the same with God. I was dating a guy and fearful that God would tell me to end the relationship. So I stopped talking to God about it. I didn't ask what he thought, I didn't tell him my worries and joys. I took my relationship off the table. It wasn't long before I felt distant from God, not because he had gone anywhere but because I had.

It was time to put that relationship back on the table. To tell God there was no area of my life where he couldn't speak, challenge, change or direct. I realized I didn't have anything to fear. God is good and God is love. Anything he would ever say to me would always be out of love and for my good.

Is there anything in your life that is 'off the table'? Any area where you won't let God go? Maybe it's a relationship, an addiction, your plans or your dreams. Know that he is good and can be trusted. Consciously give him access all areas again today.

Ali

30 AUG

Your beauty and love chase after me
every day of my life.
I'm back home in the house of God
for the rest of my life.

Psalm 23.6, *The Message*

IN THE SILENCE

Recently, one of my friends was told she had cancer. She was so confused and disappointed with God, she didn't have the words to know what to say to him. So she told me she would make a cup of coffee and go and sit in her bedroom in the silence, and just be there with him. Slowly she found words to say. She told him what she thought and he comforted her and gave her the strength for the day.

If you're feeling lost and unsure about your future, find a quiet place and sit in the silence with God. He wants to meet you there.

01SEP

WORLD CHANGER

Sometimes we think that the only people who can change the world are the people with lots of power and lots of influence. Yes, they absolutely *can* change the world, but actually most of the time the people that radically change situations or events are individual people choosing to live their individual lives differently.

Think about Anne Frank — she wrote a diary during the Second World War. She was a Jewish girl and all she did was write a diary about life as a Jewish girl while the Nazis wanted to kill her and her family. That's all she did: one girl, one diary, and it's become one of the bestselling books because she lived differently. Anne wasn't bitter, she wasn't angry and she chose to love.

Think about Malala: in that moment when she stood up and took a bullet through her head, I don't suppose she was thinking, 'I'm going to change the world.' She just did the next thing in love and courage.

I think being a world changer is simply doing the next thing you're about to do and going about your life as usual, but doing it authentically and putting your whole heart and soul behind it. Being a world changer is doing everything with love; that's how you change the world.

Rachel

02 SEP

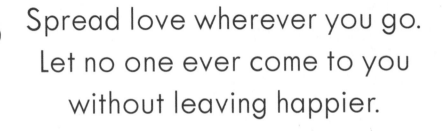

Spread love wherever you go.
Let no one ever come to you
without leaving happier.

Mother Teresa

03 SEP

VIOLATED

It was an autumn evening in the city of London and I was squished in my seat on a busy tube train. Suddenly I felt the guy next to me brush his hand down the side of my leg. It made me jump and shuffle further away from him, I thought he must have been straightening out his jacket and done it by accident. But then again, less than a minute later, his hand brushed down my thigh. I froze. Surely he's doing this by mistake? What's he doing? While these questions ran through my head, he did it a third time. I jumped up and without even thinking about it I ran off the train, which was just about to leave the station. As the doors closed behind me, I was at an unknown station but with a familiar feeling — violation.

Violation — the feeling I had at 13 years old when a man called me over to his van. I thought he was asking for directions, but he wasn't — his words violated me. It was the same feeling I had in the club when the guy tried to put his hand up my dress. The feeling I had on that train platform was the same feeling I had when the stranger on the bridge whispered something incredibly explicit into my ear as he passed me. Violated.

I didn't tell anyone about the times it happened to me because I thought it was just something I had to put up with, being a young woman — but do you know what? It's not.

You do not have to accept unwanted behaviour or contact. We need to call it out for what it is — sexual assault and harassment. If anyone touches you or intimidates you sexually, report it, make some noise about it, tell someone! Take down number plates, call the police, tell the person behind the bar about the guy that touched you, get him removed. Let's report unwanted contact because it's not just part of being a young woman, it's a crime.

Today, let's stand in unity with other girls and women, and say no to sexual harassment.

↑ ↑ 04 SEP ↑ ↑

So, chosen by God for this new life of love, dress in the wardrobe God picked out for you: compassion, kindness, humility, quiet strength, discipline. Be even-tempered, content with second place, quick to forgive an offense. Forgive as quickly and completely as the Master forgave you. And regardless of what else you put on, wear love. It's your basic, all-purpose garment. Never be without it.

Colossians 3.12–14, *The Message*

05 SEP

If you see
someone without
a smile, give
them yours.

06 SEP

THE HALF-TIME TALK

I write this on the train into London. I'm about to go to a big meeting with lots of clever, well-educated people. I'm nervous, I can feel myself shaking from my core. I'm scared that I won't fit in or know what to say. So I've decided to give myself a bit of a talking to. Here goes:

> *You are exactly who you should be. You can walk into today knowing that God has you exactly where he wants you. You are loved, cared for and gifted in your own individual way.*
>
> *Do not fear the opinions of those around you. Do not be silenced by the worry of what they may or may not think. Do not be held back by these constant concerns about your size, your style and your ability. Shine your light as you walk and as you talk today, learn from others, make a friend and remember, be yourself! Let confidence rise in you because God has given you all that you need for today. And don't forget, enjoy it!*

Do you ever feel like me? Ducking your head, heart racing because you wonder what they're thinking about you? Well, maybe that little pep talk is something you could to say to yourself too. It's my gift to you: say it regularly, say it out loud, say it in the quiet of your heart *but* believe it and let it change the way you walk around and how you live your life.

07 SEP

FEARFUL

Recently, I visited a coffee shop to write. After settling down and ordering myself a drink, out of the corner of my eye I noticed a spider on the wall.

Now, here's probably a good time to tell you that I'm terrified of spiders and in that moment I was paralysed — I couldn't think straight and my heart was racing so fast. I was finally able to get the manager to deal with the spider situation and felt so much better afterwards.

This situation (although embarrassing for me) taught me something about fear. Fear paralyses us and stops us from doing what we're here for. Maybe, like me, it's spiders stopping you from writing, or maybe it's the fear of failure stopping you from trying, or the fear of rejection causing you to keep your distance from other people. Is there something you're fearful of? Something that's paralysing you and stopping you from doing what you're here for?

When we feel fearful about a situation, it's actually really helpful to ask for someone's help. If you're feeling scared about anything at all, big or small, take a step today to find someone to share it with.

08 SEP

Be kind and compassionate
to one another, forgiving
each other, just as in Christ
God forgave you.

Ephesians 4.32

09 SEP

WORLD SUICIDE PREVENTION DAY

Darkness is my closest friend.
Psalm 88.18

I wonder if you've ever felt like that? As if the light feels scary because you only know darkness? The person who wrote this psalm has known this feeling and yet, even in the depths of despair, he or she knows that we can take those feelings to God.

God's not scared of our feelings — however dark they are.

Nothing we feel is ever too dark to be shared, whether it's with a friend, a parent, a youth worker or even down the phone to a helpline. It might feel as though darkness is your only friend, but that's a lie — talk about your darkness and you might find you catch a glimpse of the light.

Darkness thrives on silence — so we have to break that silence and talk about how we're feeling, even if we're feeling like giving up.

Rachael

10 SEP

Be strong and courageous. Do not be afraid; do not be discouraged, for the LORD your God will be with you wherever you go.

Joshua 1.9

11 SEP

GOOD FEEDBACK

When we post things on social media, we take our wonderful uniqueness, our beauty and fragile developing sense of self, and we offer ourselves up to the world. We don't know these people, they don't care about us and yet we allow them to have so much power and control over our lives. You'll get some great feedback, but you'll also get some brutal, horrible, damaging feedback (usually from people who are hurt and so they want to hurt you too).

We need to be very very careful that we don't allow people that kind of control. Before you upload anything, make sure that you have people in your life in your offline world who really understand you and that you can really take on board the good stuff that they say about you.

We need to get feedback from people who *really* care about us. If something someone has said has deflated you, take it to a person you trust and ask, 'Someone has said this about me, is it true? What do you think?' Don't sit there with it and let it take root in your life; don't let it grow in you.

(Remember, you are able to make decisions to protect yourself and choose whether to be vulnerable. Sometimes you learn the hard way, but remember it's always always possible to take yourself off an account or block somebody.)

Rachel

Find a place to
stop and
be quiet.

13 SEP

SIMPLY PRAY

I don't know what you think about when you hear the word 'prayer'. Is prayer something you're familiar with? Or does it conjure up ideas of sitting in a cold stone church or kneeling beside your bed using words like 'thee' and 'thou'?

There have been times in the past that I haven't prayed because I haven't really known how to. I felt as though there was a special formula, special words — and I didn't know what they were.

Then I read this amazing bit in the Bible that says this:

> Here's what I want you to do: Find a quiet, secluded place so you won't be tempted to role-play before God. Just be there as simply and honestly as you can manage.

And then it goes on to say this:

> This is your Father you are dealing with, and he knows better than you what you need. With a God like this loving you, you can pray very simply.
> Matthew 6.6–7, The Message

Pray with simplicity. Just be there as simply and as honestly as you can. What a relief! We don't need clever words or a special formula to pray! God just wants to spend time with us.

Is there anything you would like to share with him today?

Like the joy of the sea coming home to shore, may the relief of laughter rise in your soul.

John O'Donohue, *To Bless the Space Between Us*

15 SEP

GOD-GIVEN PASSIONS

A lot of the time, you might find yourself asking the question, 'What am I supposed to do with my life?' It is a question that fills us with confusion, doubt and frustration.

But in answering this question, I think we need to first ask ourselves, 'What am I passionate about?' I believe that God has created us with innermost passions and desires, and often these can be an indicator for God's plan for our life. I believe that God has created us to love what we do and I believe that our passions are meant to be adventurously explored.

Ask God to show you how he wants you to use your God-given passions for his glory today.

Jessie

16 SEP

You're blessed when you feel you've lost what is most dear to you. Only then can you be embraced by the One most dear to you.

Matthew 5.4, *The Message*

17 SEP

Rescue me, Lord, and hold
me in your loving arms.

18 SEP

KEEP AN EYE ON YOUR HEART

Above all else guard your heart, for everything you do flows from it.
Proverbs 4.23

Do you know what's going on in your heart? The Bible says that we are to keep an eye on it as a top priority. Above all else we must guard — keep a careful watch on — the condition of our heart.

How do we do this? We look for symptoms. Signs that not everything is as it should be . . .

Hungry heart	Raging insecurity, over-the-top need for affirmation and attention, looking for comfort in the wrong things
Fearful heart	Scared to try new things, to trust, to take risks
Hopeless heart	A general feeling that things can't and won't get better
Wounded heart	Feeling let down or rejected, scared to love and be loved
Hardening heart	Uncaring towards or critical of others.

When we see signs that our hearts aren't doing great then we simply need to come back to God, who made our hearts in the first place and who makes our hearts whole again. To take a moment to rest and receive his peace, affirmation, hope, love and joy.

Everything we do flows from the condition of our hearts. So let's keep an eye on them and keep coming back to the One who loves us and repairs our hearts.

Ali

19 SEP

Stop looking down and seeing changes that need to be made, Look down and see a beauty that will never fade.

20 SEP

CONTENT WHATEVER THE CIRCUMSTANCES

I've learned by now to be quite content whatever my circumstances. I'm just as happy with little as with much, with much as with little. I've found the recipe for being happy whether full or hungry, hands full or hands empty. Whatever I have, wherever I am, I can make it through anything in the One who makes me who I am.

Philippians 4.12–14, *The Message*

21 SEP

YOU ALL RIGHT?

Now I'm not going to name names, but this morning I saw someone I knew and I said, 'Morning! How are you?' And this was her reply: 'Oh, not too good, I've actually got pretty bad bowel problems.'

Well, I was completely shocked!! I said something like, 'Oh no, I hope you feel much better soon!' and walked off, thinking, 'My goodness, talk about over-sharing!' As I wandered into town, I mulled over what she had said and I realized that she was simply answering my question, 'How are you?'

I live in Essex and the way we greet one another is to say, 'You all right?' and even if I'm having the worst of days I'll reply with, 'Yeah, you all right?' But I love the idea of honestly sharing how we're feeling. OK, maybe revealing that we have embarrassing bowel problems is a bit brave, but so often we keep ourselves to ourselves when we're feeling down or having a bad day. When we bottle up our feelings, it can begin to eat away at us.

Do you need to open up more to the people around you? Try to give an honest answer the next time someone asks how you are. It can be nerve-wracking sharing if we're struggling, but lean on the people around you — they care!

22 SEP

Give me the courage to show
up and let myself be seen.

Brené Brown, research professor,
author and speaker

23 SEP

IN YOUR EYES

When I was 19, I went on tour to the USA with the band I was in. We spent six weeks travelling around performing at all sorts of different venues, including schools. We were planning on doing exactly the same as we did in schools across the UK – we'd perform four songs and then I'd share a message about faith and how much God loves them, only . . . when we arrived in the States we were asked not to mention faith at all in schools.

I was gutted as someone told me about God's love for me when I was 12 and it's been the most amazing adventure ever since. So after performing a couple of songs in the first school, I stood on the stage and spoke about our identities and not trying to be anyone else but yourself. As we finished and stepped off the stage, a teacher came up to me and said, 'Thank you so much, I'm a Christian too!' *Ahh*, my heart started racing! In a panic, I said, 'Ohh no! Did I say something about faith in God??' and her reply was such a surprise. 'No,' she said, 'I could just see it in your eyes.'

That comment was the first time I realized that when we give our lives to God and walk with him, he inhabits our whole body. In 1 Corinthians 3.16–17, it says, 'You realize, don't you, that you are the temple of God, and God himself is present in you?' (*The Message*). How awesome is that?? We carry God's love and presence wherever we go, and we don't always have to use words – people will see him.

Ask God to fill you today with his love so that you can carry it to everyone around you. My prayer for you is that people will see his love in your eyes today and every day.

24 SEP

WHERE I AM

Father,
Where I am fearful, please give me your peace.
Where I am worried, please give me your reassurance.
Where I am weak, please give me your strength.
Where I am sad, please give me your joy.
Where I am lost, please give me direction.
Where I am alone, please remind me that you are there.

25 SEP

GROW A NEW HABIT

If you had to name your bad habits, you probably wouldn't find it too hard — biting nails, leaving homework till the last minute, watching TV and being on your phone *at the same time*, eating junk food . . .

But what about your good habits? Whether it's walking to school rather than taking the bus, drinking plenty of water, saving money, having an early night, flossing your teeth . . . One day you made a decision to start and now you probably don't even think about it. You just do it and it makes a difference.

Here's a great habit that we could all grow in: being thankful.

Psalm 136.1 says, 'Give thanks to the LORD, for he is good. His love endures for ever.'

And James 1.17 tells us that every good and perfect gift is from our Father.

God is good and he gives us good things. Whether it is the gift of his Son, Jesus, the gift of a new day, a beautiful view, great friends — every day there is so much to be thankful for. We can grow this good habit by starting and ending every day saying thank you to God for just three things. And when we see something beautiful, when something happens that's good, when we feel joy or peace over a certain situation, take a moment to tell him how thankful we are. It won't take long before you have grown a new habit. Why not start now?

Ali

26 SEP

I GIVE IT ALL TO YOU

Do you ever feel a bit overwhelmed by life? Sometimes there's so much to do and so much to cope with, isn't there? Next time you feel overwhelmed, I'd encourage you to try this . . .

Find a quiet place where you won't be interrupted (I've often chosen a locked bathroom!). Kneel down and then clench your fists together. Imagine that you're holding all the things that you're dealing with in your hands: you're clinging tightly to them and they're there in front of you. Now, gently open your hands and place them in front of you with your palms facing upwards. And pray this simple prayer, 'Father, I give it all to you.'

You can stay there with God in the silence for as long as you want; he will meet you there.

27 SEP

I pray that from his glorious, unlimited resources he will empower you with inner strength through his Spirit. Then Christ will make his home in your hearts as you trust in him. Your roots will grow down into God's love and keep you strong. And may you have the power to understand, as all God's people should, how wide, how long, how high, and how deep his love is. May you experience the love of Christ, though it is too great to understand fully. Then you will be made complete with all the fullness of life and power that comes from God.

Ephesians 3.16–19, *New Living Translation*

28 SEP

BE BOLD

Boldness isn't always about climbing the highest mountain
Or being the strongest or the best.
Boldness can be stepping out, being brave
Simply putting yourself to the test.

Being bold doesn't mean you're not scared!
It means that despite the fears
And the 'arrghhh I can't do it' ringing in your ears,
You take a step forward.

Boldly take off your mask and be you,
Unashamedly, entirely, wholeheartedly you.
And that takes bravery
Because so often we worry 'what will they think of me?'
But when those words echo in your mind.
That's your moment to be bold.
Being bold is raising your head up,
Allowing yourself to show up,
Speak up,
Not always telling yourself to shut up.

29 SEP

HEAR WHAT HE HAS TO SAY

When I was first exploring what it would mean for me to actually be a Christian, I used to hear people talk about 'hearing God'. I found this quite a strange concept and I wasn't fully sure what it meant. One thing I definitely did think, though, is that God speaking to *me* would never happen. I figured it was for the 'super holy' people or those at the front of church preaching and leading worship. It turns out that's not exactly what people meant when they were trying to tell me to open my ears to God.

What they meant is that God is communicating with us *all the time*. Now this doesn't always mean an audible voice (in fact, I'd say hearing God in an audible voice is pretty rare for most people!). But it could mean God speaking to you through the advice a friend gives you about a situation you're facing. It might be that you sense God's presence in some kind of way in a situation you're facing right now. God doesn't show up blaring trumpets and declaring his arrival. In fact, he wants to be involved in your day-to-day life. Just as much as he wants us to pray and call out to him for things we want and need, he wants us to take time to listen for his voice and to hear what he has to say too.

Naomi

30 SEP

EMBRACE HIS LOVE

Did you know that you can't make God love you any more or any less? You are his daughter, his prized possession and he just can't help loving you.

There's a great verse in Romans that says this:

> I'm absolutely convinced that nothing — nothing living or dead, angelic or demonic, today or tomorrow, high or low, thinkable or unthinkable — absolutely nothing can get between us and God's love because of the way that Jesus our Master has embraced us.
> Romans 8.38–39, *The Message*

His love for you is beyond what you can comprehend, it's so high and so wide and so deep. You cannot be separated from this love, but the question is, have you accepted it? Turn to face God, open your arms, embrace his love and let it transform every part of you.

YOU ARE MORE THAN JUST PRETTY

What does it really mean to be beautiful?

Society has filled this void for centuries with its own ideas and visions of beauty which people believe to be true (through magazines, social media, TV, advertising, etc.) Yet they've been wrong all along.

Beauty is not just what we look like. Beauty is not found in make-up and clothes. Beauty is not just the image staring back at us in the mirror. Beauty is about character: it's about who we are. In 1 Peter 3.3–4, it says, 'Your beauty should not come from outward adornment . . . it should be that of your inner self .'

One of my favourite reminders is this:

Girls, you are more than just pretty. You are pretty kind, pretty loving, pretty compassionate, pretty brave and pretty strong.

When we next look in the mirror or chat to a mate, let's challenge ourselves to focus more on character than outward appearance.

Jessie

02 OCT

In a world where you
can be anything,
be kind.

CHANGE

The only thing about life that doesn't change is that life changes!

It can be really difficult when we're facing changes like going to a new school or moving to a new area. Our foundations can feel as though they're on shifting sands. It's disorientating, isn't it?

I have to admit that I don't find change particularly easy to navigate, and I don't think I'm alone in that. So often it makes me question who I am and makes me wonder how I'm going to build a life that looks so different from the one I've loved and left behind.

So I look to the unchanging One – because whatever we go through, God doesn't change.

Friends might move away, parents might separate, but the Bible promises that God is the same yesterday, today and for ever.

Rachael

04 OCT

SLOW DOWN

The other day I was in a real rush — cue erratic breathing and flapping of arms. I was feeling frantic. I needed to drive two hours across London to a meeting about a film I was making, but first I *needed* coffee. It was 6 a.m. and I ran into the service station and gave my order. The moment it was in my hand I raced back to the car, jumped in, bag down, belt on, turned the key, pulled away and *splash!!* A wall of steaming liquid drenched my windscreen. I jumped out of my skin!

As the steam rose off the glass, I realized I had left my precious coffee balanced on the roof. Gaaaah. The coffee was no more.

Here's the lesson I really need to learn . . . when you rush and get stressed, it's easier to make mistakes and get things wrong.

If, like me, you have a habit of getting a bit stressed and always being in a rush, then my challenge for you today is to take a deep breath and slow down. Make a conscious effort to relax and calm your thoughts. Don't miss out on the enjoyment of today.

05 OCT

Forget the negativity you've been told,
Forget your failures.
Forget the former things,
Do not dwell on the past
But run fast, toward your goal.
Keep on keeping on.

06OCT

Suffering produces
perseverance;
perseverance, character;
and character, hope.

Romans 5.3–4

07 OCT

God is sheer mercy and grace;
not easily angered, he's rich in love.

He doesn't endlessly nag and scold,
nor hold grudges forever.

He doesn't treat us as our sins deserve,
nor pay us back in full for our wrongs.

As high as heaven is over the earth,
so strong is his love to those who fear him.

And as far as sunrise is from sunset,
he has separated us from our sins.

Psalm 103.8–12, *The Message*

Be gentle with yourself today,
you are still growing.

09 OCT

THERE'S MORE IN YOU

You are not a finished article.

That is a statement that I find incredibly freeing! It means that there is always more in us. God is never finished with us. He is always working in and through us in every situation and circumstance we're facing. There is so much untapped strength and potential in each one of us! I find it so exciting that we have so much more to realize about ourselves.

He is the potter and we are the clay — he is forever at work moulding and shaping us into the girl he had in mind when he created us.

> Yet you, LORD, are our Father.
>   We are the clay, you are the potter;
>   we are all the work of your hand.
> Isaiah 64.8

Jessie

10 OCT

If life is a journey, let's walk each other's roads, Keep each other going, and help to carry each other's loads.

11 OCT

DOING CONFIDENCE

Sometimes we think that confidence is something you're born with, but it's not. Confidence is not a feeling, it's an action, so if you think, 'One day I'll feel confident,' I can tell you now, that won't happen. The only way to *feel* confident is to *do* confidence.

Confidence is a result of experience. Take a situation where somebody at school says to you, 'I want you to go around to every single class and give a notice saying that there's going to be a collection taken tomorrow.' The first time you walk into a class you're feeling like, 'Arrgh, this is going to be awful, I don't want to do this! What if I walk in and I've tucked my skirt into my knickers?!' But let's say you go into that first class, give your notice and you survive! Nobody laughs at you, and you walk out of that class and think, 'All right, that wasn't too bad.' So, you go down the corridor into the next class, you give your notice and again nobody laughs. The more you experience that actually the worst doesn't happen, then the more your confidence grows, to the point that, even if you then walk into a class and someone makes a silly comment, you can brush it off, because actually you know that most of the time when you step out it's all right.

If you want to grow in confidence (which we all do!), give yourself time to do confident things and challenge yourself to do hard stuff. Start somewhere small and safe — with something that you think you could probably just about manage — and then take it from there, slowly building up your confidence. When you build up your experience, it helps you to realize that 'I can do this!' It will get to the point where you will be able to do anything, because your experience tells you that whether it goes well or whether it totally flops, actually it's all right! You can pick yourself up and try it again.

So if you want to get more confident, expose yourself to situations where you can grow.

Rachel

She who kneels
before God can
stand before anyone.

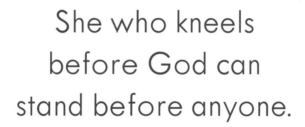

13 OCT

THE FRUITS OF THE SPIRIT

Now if you've never heard about the 'fruits of the Spirit' then it may sound like some new juice drink, but it's not. The Bible talks about the qualities we can grow in our lives, just like fruit.

I imagine it like this: those that follow Jesus are like trees planted by a stream of water. (In fact, it says this in Psalm 1 — check it out!) And like those trees, we're growing and soaking up God's rich goodness, nourishing ourselves with his love and his words and being fed by his Holy Spirit.

In Galatians, it says this: 'But what happens when we live God's way? He brings gifts into our lives, much the same way that fruit appears in an orchard' (Galatians 5.22, *The Message*).

I love that! And it goes on to tell us about the gifts that he can grow in our life if we let him . . .

> *But the fruit of the Spirit is love, joy, peace, forbearance, kindness, goodness, faithfulness, gentleness and self-control.*
> Galatians 5.22–23

Aren't they such amazing things to grow? To be honest, I think I need more of all of them. Is there anything you would like to grow more of? Then let your roots go down deep into God.

14 OCT

NON-SLIP SOUL GRIP

I once had a pair of winter boots. I loved them but they had one major flaw: the soles had no grip whatsoever. Every time I wore them I nearly ended up on my backside. After months of this instability, I turned to Google for help. Was there a way to turn my boots non-slip?

The first idea sounded perfect. A product in a can — Quick Fix Sole Grip. All I would have to do is spray it on, but sadly it wasn't available in this country. Back to Google I went and found the suggestion to scratch and scrape the bottom of the shoes until the surface was no longer smooth. I took a knife and set to it. It was hard! It took some muscle but it worked. My boots are no longer an accident waiting to happen.

How do we stay upright when life bowls a googly? We would love a quick fix faith grip that means no matter what we face we aren't floored by life's flaws. But it doesn't work like that. If we want to walk secure, we have to do the (sometimes) hard graft of digging into the word of God.

In the Bible, we see the promises, the character and the love of a God who doesn't change. When we hold on to these, we find that the ground under our feet is secure even when life isn't. Why not find some time to read and hold on to just one of these amazing truths today?

Here are some suggestions to get you started:

* Romans 8.28
* Ephesians 3.20
* Isaiah 46.4.

Ali

15OCT

If God brings you to it,
he will bring you through it.

16 OCT

CONTROL OVER MY THOUGHTS

When I think back to school life, what really stands out to me is how much I disliked myself. Trips to the mirrors in the school bathroom or glimpses of my face as I walked down the corridor reminded me regularly that I felt like rubbish and I was rubbish. It turns out that that thought process itself is total *rubbish*.

Although those thoughts haven't altogether disappeared with time, I've realized more and more how much of a waste of time they are! *And* I also realized how I can actually have control over my thoughts. The thoughts I have about myself, and the thoughts you have about yourself, are just as important as the thoughts you have about others.

I would never tell anyone else that he or she is rubbish, so why do I talk to myself in that way?

The small positives that we tell ourselves about who we are will gradually start to take the place of the rubbish thoughts that we have. God's word helps us to see the reality about who we are, and his thoughts are the ones we need to listen to and hold on to.

Jessie

17OCT

PRECIOUS

When I was 15, I had a very significant run-in with my dad. I remember the night quite vividly.

I had got into the habit of leaving my parents' house to go out with friends wearing one outfit and then changing into something I thought was 'more sexy' when I got to my friends' house. The more I did this, the more risks I took, and one evening I thought, 'What the heck, I can sneak out the front door without being caught!'

All was going well until the unexpected happened. I had my hand on the front door latch when all of a sudden my dad (who must have been listening out for me) threw open the lounge door and caught me sneaking out of the house in full Lycra® splendour! I shut my eyes and waited for my dad to lay into me . . . But he surprised me.

He just looked at me and said, 'Rachel, you're my best and only daughter. I'm really proud of you and hope you have a great night.'

That was it! I was stunned. No shouting, no lecture, no grounding. I was free to go!

As I walked out of the house, something inside me clicked. I looked at what I was wearing and felt as cheap as the fabric it was made of. I turned round, went back to my room and changed into something else.

I still had times when I wore really revealing clothes. I still wanted the boys to look at me. But from that moment on I knew for sure that my dad thought I was beautiful and I didn't need to prove myself to anyone else.

God your Father created you to be beautiful — and that's what you are! He made your heart, mind and soul — and he also created your body. You don't need to keep it hidden away under layers of cardigans or tracksuits. You also don't need to put it on display to entice boys to take a second look at you. Instead, God wants you to accept, appreciate and value your body.

Rachel

18 OCT

You're blessed when you're content with just who you are — no more, no less. That's the moment you find yourselves proud owners of everything that can't be bought.

Matthew 5.5, *The Message*

19OCT

WHO ARE YOU IN YOUR HOUSE?

I used to slam doors at home, stomp around and be the drama queen of the house. I've stopped slamming doors and stomping around but . . . the drama queen thing? Well, I'm working on that.

I would storm around my house and make things pretty difficult for my parents. I never gave a second thought to how it made them feel — they were my parents, they just had to deal with it. I never thought of the fact that my parents were actually people, that my mum and dad were more than just my mum and dad, they had feelings, they felt tired, they were doing their best.

How do you treat your parents? Do you treat them well? Or are you a handful like I was? I made life tough for my parents and I regret that now, I'd like to take back the drama and the stomping around and be kinder to them.

Who are you in your house? Are you the drama queen? The arguer? Perhaps you're the moaner. Or are you the peacemaker? The laugher? The helper?

Who do you *think* you should be? Try hard to be that person.

20 OCT

Our faith can
move mountains.

See Matthew 17.20

21 OCT

GREED

I recently heard someone speak on the subject of greed. When the talk was first beginning I thought, 'I'm not a greedy person, this isn't really going to apply to me.' As I heard more and more, however, my ears were pricking up and I was thinking, 'Hold on, that sounds like me!'

The lady was speaking about never being satisfied and always wanting more. I've realized recently that whenever I get a spare minute I'm always on my phone, shopping! Sometimes I buy things but mostly I just browse and daydream about what I'd like.

What a waste of time!!

Greed is a really good way to describe it. I've got clothes, shoes and a house filled with everything I need – I don't *need* more and yet deep down I *want* more.

Do you ever find yourself, like me, wanting the newer, the bigger and the better? Why is that? I think it's partly because we live in a society that encourages us to want more and more stuff! There are always newer versions of everything. The dictionary defines greed as an 'intense and selfish desire for something, especially wealth, power, or food'.

So what's the opposite of greed? Well I think it's contentment, right? In Philippians, we read this:

> *I've learned by now to be quite content whatever my circumstances. I'm just as happy with little as with much, with much as with little. I've found the recipe for being happy whether full or hungry, hands full or hands empty. Whatever I have, wherever I am, I can make it through anything in the One who makes me who I am.*
> Philippians 4.12–14, *The Message*

How can we be content whether we've got a lot or a little? Paul says he has found the secret, and it's Jesus. I know it's a *huge* challenge, but let's try to not make our lives about stuff, always wanting more, defining ourselves by what we've got. Let's define ourselves by how God sees us.

22 OCT

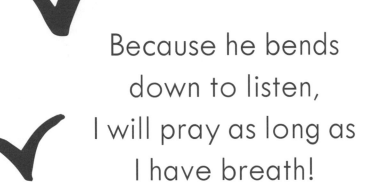

Because he bends
down to listen,
I will pray as long as
I have breath!

Psalm 116.2, *New Living Translation*

23 OCT

There isn't one definition of beauty. Beauty isn't the size of your jeans, the condition of your skin, the glossiness of your hair or a number on the scales.

Your beauty is in your eyes, your laugh, your hopes for the future, your passion and your talents.

Your beauty shines out when you are just being you.

24 OCT

What is impossible with people
is possible with God.

25OCT

Be especially careful when you are trying to be good so that you don't make a performance out of it. It might be good theater, but the God who made you won't be applauding. When you do something for someone else, don't call attention to yourself. You've seen them in action, I'm sure — 'playactors' I call them — treating prayer meeting and street corner alike as a stage, acting compassionate as long as someone is watching, playing to the crowds. They get applause, true, but that's all they get. When you help someone out, don't think about how it looks. Just do it — quietly and unobtrusively. That is the way your God, who conceived you in love, working behind the scenes, helps you out.

Matthew 6.1–4, *The Message*

26 OCT

WANTING FREEDOM

When I was 19, I went into a women's prison in Manchester to speak at an Alpha Course. To say that I was nervous is an understatement. As the last few chairs were being filled, I felt my head emptying of everything I had planned to say. I was frantically searching my brain for the well-rehearsed talk I had prepared. Gone. Totally gone. I was introduced and then it was down to me.

Silence.

I could hear my heart pumping and I was convinced that everyone else could hear it too. So I prayed silently and quickly: 'God, please help me to say what you want!' The next ten minutes were a bit of a blur, but when I finished speaking I whispered to my friend Lucy, 'Was that all right? What was I talking about?' And to my horror she said, 'Meg, you talked about freedom.'

Freedom!? Well that's a sensitive subject to bring up with a load of prisoners! It turns out I'd spoken to the ladies about a verse in the Bible that says, 'So if the Son sets you free, you will be free indeed' (John 8.36) and shared about the freedom you get from giving your life to God.

I don't know where you are right now but I want to ask you: is there something you need freedom from? Do you feel trapped by your thoughts or by your past? Jesus offers you complete freedom and life in abundance. It's yours for the taking — all you need to do is open your hands and receive it. If there's something that's led you to feel trapped, then pray this prayer with me:

> *Jesus, I need freedom today.*
> *As I open my hands, I let go.*
> *I give you permission to release the chains that have bound me for so long.*
> *Release my mind from the negative thoughts,*
> *Release me from the painful memories of the past.*
> *Let freedom flood my heart like light flooding a dark room.*
> *Thank you.*

27 OCT

Look for the best
in yourself,
not the worst.

THANKFULNESS JOURNAL

Something that has definitely helped me in the past is keeping a thankfulness journal. Each day I've written down one thing that I'm grateful for. It might be as simple as 'the sunshine' or 'clean tap water' but in the days that are hard it's encouraging to look back and be reminded that there's always something to feel grateful for.

What are you thankful for today?

29 OCT

Life is too short
to spend it at war
with yourself.

BIG QUESTIONS: DO GHOSTS EXIST?

A recent YouGov survey reported that more Brits believe in ghosts than a Creator God. But what does God say about ghosts?

Numerous passages in the Bible imply that death leads only to an afterlife, with no reference to ghostly visitations (Hebrews 9.27; 1 Corinthians 15). But there are a few instances of potential paranormal activity.

In the book of Job, one of Job's friends, Eliphaz, claims to have been visited by a ghostly figure: 'A spirit glided past my face, and the hair on my body stood on end. It stopped, but I could not tell what it was. A form stood before my eyes, and I heard a hushed voice' (Job 4.15–16). Was Eliphaz making it up? Was he visited by a dead person? Was it an evil spirit? Some have suggested that Elijah and Moses appeared as ghosts alongside Jesus at the Transfiguration (Matthew 17), and Jesus himself was mistaken for a ghost on numerous occasions (Matthew 14; Luke 24).

There is an understanding of ghosts in the Bible, but the general consensus seems to be that, whether they are evil or merely souls with 'unfinished business', these spirits, and the power to summon them, are not to be trifled with (Ephesians 6). Passages such as 1 Samuel 28 and Deuteronomy 18 seem to explicitly condemn activities like divination and consulting mediums.

While some 'ghostly visits' may be explained away by an overactive imagination, a trick of the light or part of a grieving process, many people claim to have seen a ghost, so maybe we shouldn't entirely dismiss their existence.

Why are we drawn to spooky things? Where does our fascination with things outside our understanding and control come from? Were we, perhaps, created with an innate knowledge that there's more to life than meets the eye?

Around Halloween it's easy to be fearful of ghosts. But one thing is clear throughout the Bible: no matter how powerful other spirits are, we needn't worry because nothing is as powerful as God's love for us (Romans 8.38–39).

Ruth

31 OCT

THANK YOU, ERIC

Once upon a time (all great stories start with that, right?) I met a lovely old man called Eric in a café. Eric was 92 and I chatted to him about his childhood, his experiences in the war and his family. Before he left, I said to him, 'You're obviously slightly (!) older than I am: what advice would you give me for life?' And do you know what he said? Two simple but powerful words . . .

Help others.

Wow. We said our goodbyes, and as he walked out I felt really emotional — I doubt I'll ever see Eric again but I was inspired by his attitude towards life. He'd learnt the beautiful lesson that life isn't all about us. It's so very easy for us to settle for a selfish life and to be focused on ourselves, but a life lived helping and caring for others is so much fuller and more fruitful, and Eric had discovered that.

What great words for us to remember today, to help others. Thank you, Eric!

01 NOV

Let all that you do be
done with love.

LIVE FREELY

Jesus said,

> Come to me, all you who are weary and burdened, and I will give you rest. Take my yoke upon you and learn from me, for I am gentle and humble in heart, and you will find rest for your souls. For my yoke is easy and my burden is light.
> Matthew 11.28–30

You don't have to carry shame or guilt around with you. Whether it's the first, tenth or thousandth time you've messed up, God is there for you.

Lay your burdens down before God and find relief for your weary soul.

0.3 NOV

LOOK, LOOK WHAT GOD HAS DONE!

There's a story in the Bible about a teenage girl called Rhoda which really inspires me. Probably a refugee, she becomes a servant girl in a family who have just converted to Christianity. One night, all these Christians are praying for a really important person called Peter, one of the most important people in the early church. Peter has been arrested and these Christians are really afraid that he will be murdered. It's a great story where they're all praying that God will release Peter from jail – and, basically, God does!

It's brilliant! This angel bumps Peter out of the prison and walks him through the gates. There's this wonderful moment where Peter is banging on the door of the house and Rhoda, the servant girl, looks out of the window and she's like '*Woww!* It's Peter!' She's now caught between these two realities. On the one hand she's got people saying, 'Rhoda, stop bothering us! We need to pray for Peter.' And she's like 'But I can see him, he's at the door!'

Rhoda is absolutely there, right in the middle of the drama of this amazing event. She gets to open the door on this incredible thing that God has done, and that really inspired me. I read that when I was younger and I thought, 'I often feel a bit invisible, I often feel powerless, I often feel as if I need to be more like this and more like that.' But it was Rhoda who got to open the door on the great miracle that God had done and shout, 'Look, look what God has done!' and that has inspired me to want to always be in the front seat and asking, 'God, where are you doing amazing stuff?' I want to see it, I want to be there, I want to open the door and to say to others, 'Look, look! Can you see what God is already doing? He's already here.'

Rachel

04 NOV

Give me new eyes so that I can see
And accept that you made me beautifully.

WHAT'S IN A NAME?

Do you know what your name means? If I look up 'Ruth', all sorts of things pop up, from 'distress or grief' (oh dear) to 'companion' and 'vision of beauty' (I'll take that one!).

But aside from our birth name, we're also called other names: 'stupid', 'ugly', 'boring'. What names have you had spoken over you?

In the last book of the Bible, Revelation, God speaks to seven churches. One of these, the church of Philadelphia, was in a place where Christians experienced persecution. Their city was also prone to terrible earthquakes and had been completely destroyed at least twice. Each time the city was rebuilt, it was renamed in honour of the leader who helped pay for its restoration. After the first earthquake in AD 17, Philadelphia was renamed 'Caesar's new city'. But in Revelation 3.12, Jesus promises his suffering Church an infinitely greater name: 'The city of my God, the new Jerusalem'.

If you feel your life is hard work, you're falling apart and are in serious need of restoration, you can rest assured that, like the church in Philadelphia, God sees your ruins and promises to rebuild you and give you a new name.

God's words to this struggling church in Philadelphia echo something earlier in the Bible. In the Old Testament, God says this to his harassed people:

> You'll get a brand-new name
>   straight from the mouth of GOD . . .
> No more will anyone call you Rejected,
>   and your country will no more be called Ruined.
> You'll be called Hephzibah.
> Isaiah 62.2, 4, *The Message*

You will no longer be called 'rejected' or 'ruined'. You will be called 'Hephzibah', which means 'my delight is in her'. No matter what you think about yourself, God delights in you. Regardless of what names have been spoken over you, either by others or by yourself, God speaks a new name over you. He says that you are his delight.

Ruth

06 NOV

GOD, my shepherd!
    I don't need a thing.
You have bedded me down in lush meadows,
    you find me quiet pools to drink from.
True to your word,
    you let me catch my breath
    and send me in the right direction.
Even when the way goes through Death Valley,
I'm not afraid
    when you walk at my side.
Your trusty shepherd's crook
    makes me feel secure.

Psalm 23.1–4, *The Message*

07 NOV

BE PATIENT WITH ME

As I write this, it's early in the morning and there's a new person working in my local coffee shop — it sounds as if it's her first day. Her eyes are wide as she tries to take in all the information that's being given to her. She looks a bit shaky and I just want to give her a massive hug! Her colleague has left her to work the tills and there's a long queue forming because it's taking her a while to serve each customer. I can see some people in the queue getting restless and rolling their eyes; all I want to do is get a megaphone and announce to the shop, 'It's her first day!!' She could really do with a little badge that says, 'Be patient with me, I'm new here.'

In fact, we could all do with a badge, couldn't we? Today, mine would read, 'Be patient with me, I'm not sleeping very well.' What would yours say?

We never really know what the people around us are coping with, so I simply want to encourage you to be patient with people you meet today, because you don't know what internal struggle they're facing.

08 NOV

So, what do you think? With God on our side like this, how can we lose? If God didn't hesitate to put everything on the line for us, embracing our condition and exposing himself to the worst by sending his own Son, is there anything else he wouldn't gladly and freely do for us?

Romans 8.31–32, *The Message*

09NOV

You're a whole lot of lovely.

10 NOV

✘ WHO ARE YOU REMEMBERING?

At the going down of the sun and in the morning, We will remember them.
Robert Laurence Binyon, 'For the Fallen'

You may be a pacifist (against war in every situation), you may think war should only ever be a last resort or you may not have a strong opinion either way. Regardless of our beliefs, Remembrance Day is a good time to look back and remember.

Remember the fallen

My dad was an army chaplain, so he spent a lot of time remembering brave colleagues and helping to support their families and friends. You might not personally know anyone in the armed forces, but we can still support and pray for those who have been affected by conflict around the world.

Remember Jesus' sacrifice

Our soldiers, past and present, sacrifice their lives so we can live in freedom. Likewise, Jesus willingly chose to lay down his life so we can be free. Hebrews says: 'Christ offered himself as a sacrifice that is good for ever . . . By his one sacrifice he has for ever set free from sin the people he brings to God' (Hebrews 10.12, 14, *Contemporary English Version*).

Remember God's help

There's a story in 1 Samuel 7 that speaks of Israel's bloody battle with the Philistines. So far, so spectacularly gruesome. But then we get to verse 12. Having defeated the Philistines, Samuel (Israel's prophet) lays down a stone and calls it Ebenezer. Far from meaning a grumpy, Christmas-hating miser, this Hebrew word means 'stone of help'. While he is laying the stone down, Samuel says this: 'Thus far the LORD has helped us.' It is there to remind the Israelites of God's help in the past so they can be confident of his help in the future.

Has God ever helped you? Have you felt his presence in the midst of your darkest moments? What would you like him to help you with today?

This Remembrance Day, let's raise our remembrance stones of help. Let's be thankful for the sacrifices of the fallen. And let's remember the greatest sacrifice of all, Jesus, who has for ever given us freedom.

Ruth

11 NOV

God can do anything, you know — far more than you could ever imagine or guess or request in your wildest dreams! He does it not by pushing us around but by working within us, his Spirit deeply and gently within us.

Ephesians 3.20, *The Message*

12NOV

In the middle of it all,
The laughter and the tears,
The highs, lows and fears,
He's there and he cares.

In the middle of it all,
The worry and pain,
When it'll never be the same,
He's there and he cares.

In the middle of it all,
The laughter and conversation,
The disappointment and frustration,
He's there and he cares.

In the middle of it all
He *is* there, in the middle of it all.

GOOD NEWS

I find it so hard to watch the news. There's so much pain, sadness, death and evil in the world. (Stick with me, this will get more positive, I promise!)

Oh, let's just skip to the hopeful part now. The hopeful part is . . . you!

Yes, you are someone who can bring hope to the world around you, someone who can do good, lift someone's mood, make someone smile and ultimately change the world. Right now, where you are, you can change your town.

Can you imagine if one by one around the world we make it our own personal mission to be peacemakers and to love those around us? We would start a revolution! A movement of people dedicated to changing the world.

God's love for us is good news. Let's receive his love and then spread it around us and change our communities. Are you with me? Let's start today.

14 NOV

BEING STILL

'Be still and know that I am God' — they're famous words in the Bible, and yet I for one am not particularly good at being still. Being still isn't about staying still and doing nothing. It's remembering that we are valuable just as we are.

There is nothing we can do, say or think that will stop us being human and being valuable. We don't need to get the highest grades, be a pro sportswoman or a top-level pianist to be valuable. Take a moment to let that sink in.

There is nothing we should do or can do to earn God's love — we are as loved when we're fast asleep as when we're working late into the night. Remind yourself of that today; in the quiet moments and the chaotic moments, you can be still and know that you are loved and that God is king over everything.

Rachael

15 NOV

Protect me, Father, from the
pressure of today.

16 NOV

PRESENT YOUR REQUESTS TO GOD

In that moment when you feel the worries and the anxious thoughts rising and you sense they could take over, imagine pressing a pause button on the moment. Then, in the silence of your heart, share your thoughts and feelings with God; he wants to replace them with his incredible peace.

Do not be anxious about anything, but in every situation, by prayer and petition, with thanksgiving, present your requests to God. And the peace of God, which transcends all understanding, will guard your hearts and your minds in Christ Jesus.
Philippians 4.6–7

17 NOV

DILIGENT

'Diligent' is one of my favourite words. I just love its definition: 'careful and conscientious in work or effort'.

Diligence is carefully persevering, step by step, working hard to be the best you can be.

Can you work hard to be careful in the way you speak to your parents?

Can you work harder in your efforts at school or college, right up until the end of term?

Are there friendships that you need to carefully mend by saying sorry?

Can you make a real effort to treat your brother or sister more kindly?

Being diligent is a decision, one that I'd encourage you to make today. Be aware of the people around you, especially the ones that perhaps need a little bit more support and kindness.

Today, be full of care, and persevere in your efforts and work.

18 NOV

Christ has set us free to live a free life.

Galatians 5.1, *The Message*

APPROVAL ADDICTION: PART 1

A lad came up to me after I spoke at a youth event and said to me, 'I don't know what to do. When my friend doesn't get enough likes on her photo, she cuts herself.'

It upset me so much to hear that this girl relies so heavily on feedback from others. Sadly, in this age of posting our lives online, it can be very easy for us to become addicted to gaining the approval of others.

I've definitely felt a bit rubbish in the past when I've posted a photo or status and the reaction isn't what I'd hoped for. Have you ever felt like that?

It's a bit like wearing dodgy armbands in a swimming pool. You're swimming around but they're going down and so you ask someone to blow more air into them. But after a little while, swimming about, you need inflating again so you ask someone else to blow up your armbands, only this time the person didn't blow much in and so you're sinking a bit. Up and down you go, relying on other people to keep you afloat. In a similar way, we can sometimes post images and statuses to ask others to build us up. We go from post to post, relying on others to comment on our lives and make us feel all right.

But I believe that God wants to teach us how to swim so that we're no longer relying on others to keep us afloat. Like learning to swim, we need to learn the truth about who we are, so that whether we get 3 or 300 likes, we remain unfazed and unchanged in our belief about how valuable we are.

Can you make a choice to take off those armbands and learn the truth about your God-given identity?

If you're not sure of what that truth is, check out tomorrow's texts for the day!

20 NOV

APPROVAL ADDICTION: PART 2

Sometimes we all need reminding about our value and identity – I know I do! I question myself and struggle with comparison and confidence. So, here are three amazing truths about who you are. Own them, learn them, go over and over them and say them out loud when you feel as though you're slipping under the water.

Enjoy becoming all that God has created you to be.

You are known
You have searched me, LORD,
and you know me.
You know when I sit and when I rise;
you perceive my thoughts from afar.
You discern my going out and my lying down;
you are familiar with all my ways.
Psalm 139.1, 3

You are a child of God
See what great love the Father has lavished on us, that we should be called children of God!
1 John 3.1

You are not a mistake
My frame was not hidden from you
when I was made in the secret place,
when I was woven together in the depths of the earth.
Your eyes saw my unformed body;
all the days ordained for me were written in your book
before one of them came to be.
Psalm 139.15–16

There are plenty more truths about who you are throughout this book – look out for them and let them take root in your heart.

21 NOV

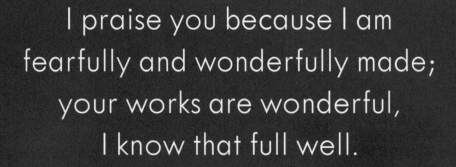

I praise you because I am
fearfully and wonderfully made;
your works are wonderful,
I know that full well.

Psalm 139.14

NOV

SUCCEEDING IN LIFE

Somewhere along the road, we pick up the idea that life is supposed to be lived successfully, that we are supposed to be successful people. The problem is that we are never told that we need to define success for ourselves. We are never told that success is subjective.

When I looked in the *Oxford English Dictionary*, these were the top two definitions of 'success':

The accomplishment of an aim or purpose.
The attainment of fame, wealth, or social status.

The first is pretty general and achievable by everyone because it's dependent upon a personal aim or purpose. But the second is pretty self-absorbed, and I think our world is slowly moving away from this as people are realizing that fame, wealth and social status don't necessarily bring happiness.

I used to be driven by monetary gain. It was exhausting! It was because I cared so much about what other people thought about me. It took quite a lot for me to create the shift in my life that was so desperately needed. If I were to define success for me nowadays, it would be the following (and maybe this will resonate with you too):

Success is living a passionate and adventurous life.

Passion is about doing something wholeheartedly, lovingly and excitedly. I want to be driven. I want to be passionate in my work and home life, in my relationships with family and friends. And I want to live adventurously. I don't want to strive for safety; I want to be driven by things that require daring, bold and courageous choices.

Knowing that this is my definition of success means that I can live confident of what I want to 'achieve' and confident about what doesn't matter to me.

How would you define success? Spend some time in prayer today asking God to reveal to you, and work with you on, your own definition of success.

Jessie

23 NOV

Rest in your
God-breathed worth.

Sarah Bessey,
Canadian author and speaker

24 NOV

WHO DOES GOD SAY YOU ARE?

One day Jesus turned to his followers and asked, 'Who do people say I am?'

When Jesus asked this, he wasn't looking for other people to give him clues as to his identity and purpose. He was already very secure and sure of who he was and what he was called to (have a read of Luke 4.16–21). The question wasn't for him, it was for them.

We are not always like Jesus! In so many ways, we live our lives asking the question, 'Who do people say I am?' Unsure of the answer, we look for our identity to be defined by the likes we get on Instagram, the people we spend time with, the way we look, the things we're good at. And the trouble with all these is that they are unreliable, they don't tell us the whole story and they won't consistently give us the true answer.

How are you defining yourself? Who do you ask about your identity and purpose? God calls you out of uncertainty and fear. He calls you by name. It's time to let go of old and inaccurate labels and take hold of his truth. Look to God and his word and you will find you are deeply loved, full of purpose, and you are his.

Ali

25 NOV

HONESTY BEFORE GOD

I was once desperately looking for somewhere to live. The viewings of properties were going badly — too expensive, too far from work, in a scary area . . . ah! I was starting to panic.

Then a friend put me in touch with a lady who was looking for a lodger. The house was a perfect distance from work, the rent was ideal, I was excited! I arrived at this huge old house, which was on its own in the middle of nowhere, and as the door creaked open an elderly lady greeted me and proceeded to show me round.

At the end of the tour of the property, she said to me, 'I'd like a lodger because if I died, I'd like someone to find me.' Ah man, my heart sank — there was no way I'd feel comfortable living there. I thanked the lady and walked down the garden path with this frustration bubbling up.

The moment I drove away in my car I exploded before God. 'What are you doing? I have nowhere to live! Do you care?' I was shouting at God and crying hysterically. I stopped the car and crumpled into a sobbing heap over the steering wheel. I was 250 miles from my home town and my family, and I felt so unsure about the future.

But God did have a plan and, soon after, I found somewhere to live. But do you know what? I think that moment in the car that day was one of the times when I've been most real with God. It was raw and real and an honest cry for help. I didn't understand what he was doing and I was cross. I've got a feeling that my faith grew that day.

I think God wants us to be ourselves before him. He knows us and loves us as we are, so we can come to him whatever state we're in. Whether you're in a good or bad state today, don't pretend before God. Say how it is and God will meet you there.

26 NOV

I WILL NOT BE AFRAID

In the past, I've been so afraid of what people think of me that I've found myself walking down the high street finding it hard to catch my breath. I'd be frantic with worried thoughts about the way other people perceive me. I still get thoughts like that, and it's so distracting. Those thoughts hold me in this momentary grip of fear — 'What do they think of me?'

Do you ever feel worried about what other people think of you?

Being afraid of people and their opinions of us can stop us from so many things: being our true selves, enjoying life, doing something that we know we're meant to do and speaking up when we have something to say.

When we look to others to give us our worth, to tell us that we're 'all right', we rely on them to make us feel valuable and loved. But what about when someone makes a negative comment about us? Suddenly we're rocked to the core because we're standing on an unreliable, unsteady foundation.

We haven't been given this precious life with so much potential to simply gain the approval of others. That's an endless, exhausting game and it's not something that God wants us to waste our time doing. The Bible tells us:

> *The Lord is my light and my salvation —*
> *whom shall I fear?*
> Psalm 27.1

When we love and fear God above anyone else, and look to him to tell us about our worth and identity, we no longer have to be afraid of people. We stand on secure ground and can walk without fear.

27 NOV

THE GOD WHO COMES LOOKING

When did you first find God's love? *Have* you found God's love?

The Bible tells us that we're only able to find God because he has already found us. He's the God who comes looking. Isn't that incredible? He doesn't hang back and wait: he woos us, draws us and melts us with his love. But he doesn't just come looking; he comes to clear every barrier that would prevent us from being loved and being love.

Spend time today asking God to reveal his love for you.

Rachel

28 NOV

WE NEED PEOPLE

Never be afraid or too ashamed to ask for help.
We *all* need help and support at times in our lives. If things
have got too much or you're struggling with something,
find someone you trust — a teacher, a parent, a friend —
and share those things with him or her. Don't live life
alone; we need people to help us.

29 NOV

MORE THAN CAPABLE

In the Bible, there's a particular passage which talks about the fact that God will never leave us or forget about us. These sound like some pretty bold statements, right? Sadly, we can often be let down by people and that can make it increasingly difficult to trust.

As difficult as it might sometimes be to trust people who have hurt us, we don't need to have these same concerns when it comes to God. It is not in his character to lie and let us down, which means we are 100 per cent safe in our trusting him. What amazing news! We can go to him with all our needs, our heart's desires, our worries, our doubt, our pain, our fear and beyond, in complete trust that he is more than capable of listening, taking on what we've said and — more than that — taking it seriously.

Trusting God is a huge aspect of the Christian life. Because, let's face it, life doesn't always go the way we plan, right? Which means that *trusting* that God knows best even (and often especially!) when we have no idea what's going on will enable us to keep going, even when the going gets tough. What has been weighing you down recently? Trust that God wants to take it and carry it for you — hand it to him today and trust him to be the bearer of your burdens — you'll feel a whole lot lighter!

Naomi

30 NOV

COBWEBS

In 2010, my friend Hannah died. A year after she died I visited a little island called Lindisfarne with my friend Sarah, just so we could get away and remember Hannah together.

We were staying with this guy Sarah knew called Geoff, who was showing us round the island. And that day, I remember, the wind was so incredibly strong, I'd never felt anything like it. Sarah and I huddled like penguins and clung on to each other as the wind tried to knock us off our feet.

Just as we reached the highest point on the island, Geoff said something that has stayed with me ever since. He said, 'This wind really does blow away the cobwebs, doesn't it?'

As I stood there, I felt I had a lot of cobwebs in my life. I felt heavy, tangled up with worries and sadness. Hannah's death had left me so many questions:

What's this all about?
Why do these horrible things happen?
What am I here for?

With Geoff's words in my mind, I turned my face into the wind, closed my eyes and silently prayed:

With this wind, God, please blow away these cobwebs inside me, clear through it all — my fears and my worries. I have so many questions, I don't understand you or what's going on, but please meet me here. I want to know you more. Thank you that you've always been close to me even when I've ignored you. Thank you for loving me even when I've messed up. Thank you for this place, for Hannah, for this wind.

Do you need to take a moment to ask God to blow away your cobwebs? He cares about you and what's going on in your life, so ask him today and he'll meet you wherever you are.

01 DEC

Desperate, I throw myself on
you:
you are my God!
Hour by hour I place my days in
your hand.

Psalm 31.14, *The Message*

STAND WITH THE ARTIST

For a long time I've had this image in my head:

It's a girl in an art gallery, standing with her face so close to a piece of artwork that her nose is almost touching it. This piece of artwork is really huge, but all she sees are a few black lines and a little section of blue — it's a blur to her because she's so close to it. 'This isn't very good,' she says.

Unbeknown to her, this piece of artwork is a masterpiece, completely priceless. But because this girl is so close to it, she can't see its awesomeness; she can't see the beauty and the incredible work of the artist because she is so close, picking it apart. Ten paces behind her stands the artist, ready to tell her all about the piece, all about its pattern and design.

I feel as though this echoes where we often stand as girls and young women. We practically have our noses to the mirror, picking ourselves apart. We scrutinize and write ourselves off as rubbish. 'This isn't very good,' we think.

We have no idea of the immense beauty before us; we are missing the breathtaking masterpiece in front of us, lovingly created by a Master Artist.

Take a step back from all your put-downs, all your self-inflicted negativity, and stand with the Artist behind you. Let him tell you about your immense value and beauty.

03 DEC

" "

Because you are the music and you write the score, would you write something beautiful to suit my voice? And I'll keep on learning to sing you your song.

'If Life Were Some Music',
Hannah Atkins,
musician

" "

04 DEC

For we live by faith,
not by sight.

2 Corinthians 5.7

05DEC

NAUGHTY OR NICE?

As the song 'Santa Claus Is Comin' to Town' tells us, Santa's hard to please. He checks the list twice, judges whether we're naughty and watches us while we sleep!

Many of us think God's like Santa. We think the Christmas story is about what we have to do to please him, but it's actually about what God did for us. He broke into the world as a baby to sort out our mess.

Romans 3.23 says: 'Everyone has sinned; we all fall short of God's glorious standard' (*New Living Translation*).

'Sin' is a bit of an old-fashioned word. It comes from a Greek word used in archery, which means 'to miss the target'.

If our target in life is God's nice list, we all fall short of it. We sin. Author Francis Spufford describes sin as 'the human tendency to muck things up' (except he uses a different word that rhymes with 'muck').

We all 'muck' things up, even if we don't mean to. Deep down, we all know we're on that naughty list, but however good we are at messing things up, God is infinitely better at mending them.

The only person who can legitimately write his name on the nice list is Jesus Christ. Yet he chose to write his name on the naughty list so we can be bumped off it. The Bible says, 'Christ suffered for our sins once for all time. He never sinned, but he died for sinners to bring you safely home to God' (1 Peter 3.18, *New Living Translation*).

Jesus coming to town is good news for everyone, not just the well-behaved. At Christmas, Jesus came into our messy world to clean it from the inside and move us on to the nice list.

Ruth

Kindness is
always beautiful.

07 DEC

I am the vine; you are
the branches. If you remain in
me and I in you, you will bear
much fruit; apart from me you
can do nothing.

John 15.5

08DEC

BIG QUESTIONS: WAS MARY A VIRGIN?

The story of Jesus' birth is told in two places in the Bible: Matthew 1 and Luke 1. Stables and random ramshackle gatherings aside, Jesus' *birth* wasn't anything out of the ordinary. It's his *conception* that is unbelievable because, quite frankly, we all know where babies come from!

Mary doesn't just accept that she's pregnant. Unsurprisingly, she asks: 'How?' Likewise, Joseph's reaction is exactly what you'd expect from a man who understood that miracles were out of the ordinary. He assumes Mary's baby has come from some dodgy activity on her part and plans to call off the engagement.

If Jesus wasn't a miracle baby, one alternative explanation is that someone other than Joseph was his dad. However, historians have pointed out that, in a small village like Nazareth, someone would have known about Mary's affair. The news would eventually have reached Joseph, and he wouldn't have stayed with her.

Maybe Matthew and Luke made it up to make Jesus seem more magical. However, there was no Jewish concept of the Messiah (the chosen one who'd deliver the Jews) being born of a virgin. The only references to virgin births at this time were in pagan stories. It seems unlikely that the Gospel writers would have written about a virgin birth unless it was actually true.

Surely Jesus being conceived without a father is impossible? Well, yes, but if you believe in God, it's arguably not too much of a jump to believe that miracles, though rare, are possible. In his book *Gunning for God*, Professor John Lennox says: 'If there is a God who created the universe, then surely there is no difficulty in believing that he could do special things.'

If Jesus was born in this miraculous way, it means he's different from every other human. The Bible says Jesus was like us but also distinct. He was both human and God. Human because he had to represent us and God because he had to be outside the problem in order to fix it. Jesus is 'Emmanuel', God with us.

Ruth

09 DEC

And let us consider how we may spur one another on towards love and good deeds.

Hebrews 10.24

10DEC

A DAUGHTER OF THE KING

I for one am tired of seeing women and girls hanging their heads in shame as though they've forgotten the most game-changing piece of news they've ever been given. Because, you know, the Bible says that you are *chosen*, which means you're precious in the sight of God. But there's some even better news than that! You're not just randomly chosen out of a bunch of people the way football teams are picked, you're chosen into God's family, which means you're his *daughter*.

I get that, right now, this all might sound a bit strange but listen up . . . God is described as 'The King of kings and the Lord of lords', which means that you're the daughter of a king! That's got quite a ring to it, right? Well, I for one think that it's high time we started acting as if we actually *believe* that our identity in God is true. We are not identified by the mistakes we've made in the past, the things which hold us back. We're actually not even defined by our families and the friends we choose to hang around with. All those things play a part, of course, but none of them affect your status as God's daughter . . . as royalty!

Naomi

11 DEC

Sing to him a new song;
    play skilfully, and shout for joy.
For the word of the LORD is right and true;
    he is faithful in all he does.
The LORD loves righteousness and justice;
    the earth is full of his unfailing love.

Psalm 33.3–5

12 DEC

BIG QUESTIONS: HOW CAN GOD ALLOW SUFFERING? PART 1

Before we look at what Christianity says, it's helpful to look at other perspectives. These are huge generalizations, but let's explore where others believe suffering comes from and what the proposed solution is.

If we take God out of the picture, suffering is just part of life. Atheist and Oxford professor Richard Dawkins says, 'The universe that we observe has precisely the properties we should expect if there is, at bottom, no design, no purpose, no evil, no good, nothing but pitiless indifference' (*River out of Eden*). Some atheists suggest that asking why we're suffering is pointless because it imposes meaning on a meaningless universe. If we remove God, humans are the only solution to suffering.

Many who follow Eastern religions believe suffering comes from being too attached to the physical world. Because many Hindus and Buddhists believe in reincarnation, this problem doesn't end when we die. We simply begin a different life of suffering.

The solution to suffering in many Eastern perspectives is to overcome earthly desires and remove ourselves from the world. In Buddhism, the purpose of meditation is to reach nirvana, which means 'extinction'. To eliminate suffering we have to get rid of our personalities and character traits – everything that makes us who we are.

If we put God back in the picture, are we suffering because of him? Many Muslims might say yes, because all events are controlled or willed by Allah. To question why you're suffering is to question Allah's will, which is blasphemy, so the solution is to bravely accept your fate and pray that Allah will alleviate the pain.

When we look at the Bible, we see that suffering is very real but also very wrong. It's not part of life as God intended. We suffer because we've rejected his good plan for our lives. When we said no to God, suffering crept in, causing a broken, painful world.

At the heart of Christianity's answer to this problem is the life, death and resurrection of Jesus, a God who suffered with us and for us and ultimately overcame suffering.

Ruth

13 DEC

BIG QUESTIONS: HOW CAN GOD ALLOW SUFFERING? PART 2

At Christmas, we often hear words from John 1 about God, 'the Word', giving life to everything. This very same God became human and 'moved into the neighbourhood' in the person of Jesus (John 1.14, *The Message*).

Jesus wasn't born in a fancy mansion in a nice part of town but in an outhouse, surrounded by dirty animals. The Christmas story shows that God doesn't stay distant. He chose to come into the mess of this world and bring light into the darkness. The shortest verse in the Bible is 'Jesus wept' (John 11.35). His best friend died and Jesus' response is exactly what ours would be. He wept. God has not left us alone in our suffering. Through Jesus, God experienced every human emotion and pain.

In *The Magician's Nephew* by C. S. Lewis, Digory's mother is dying of cancer. He asks Aslan, the lion, to cure her:

> Up till then [Digory] had been looking at the Lion's great front feet and the huge claws on them; now, in his despair, he looked up at its face. What he saw surprised him as much as anything in his whole life. For the tawny face was bent down near his own and great shining tears stood in the Lion's eyes. They were such big, bright tears compared with Digory's own that for a moment he felt as if the Lion must really be sorrier about his Mother than he was himself.

Our God weeps with us. But at his best friend's tomb, Jesus wasn't just upset; he was angry. He was raging because death and pain weren't part of creation. And if this broken world isn't as God intended it to be, it certainly isn't how he will leave it.

Because God was willing to come into our mess and help clean it up, we no longer have to do this by ourselves. The Christmas story doesn't make our pain any less severe, but it does show us that we haven't been left alone in our suffering. We have a God who grieves with us and holds us in our pain.

Ruth

14 DEC

BIG QUESTIONS: HOW CAN GOD ALLOW SUFFERING? PART 3

At the heart of the Christian faith is Jesus' broken and bleeding body. Jesus experienced every human emotion and pain, but he also experienced the ultimate suffering, the one we're most afraid of: death.

Why did Jesus have to die? Surely that's just more agony. But if we're suffering because we rebelled against God, something had to be done to put the world right. God couldn't just click his fingers and forgive us because all forgiveness costs something.

Recently, some of my friends and I were having fun decorating cheap sunglasses. I was busy pouring superglue all over myself when I heard a scream. Kelly had accidently stuck sparkly gems on Simeran's £200 sunglasses! They were completely ruined. Simeran had two choices: to make Kelly pay for another pair of sunglasses or to forgive her. If she chose to forgive, Simeran would either have to pay for new sunglasses from her own pocket or make do with the ruined ones.

Likewise, when God forgives us for messing up, there is a cost that needs to be paid. Something is still broken. Christians believe that, at the cross, Jesus paid the cost we should have paid and, in return, we receive eternal life (slightly better than new sunglasses!).

We determine the worth of most things by how much we're willing to pay for them. The cheap glasses cost 50p. They were worth hardly anything. Simeran's cost £200. They were (before they were ruined!) worth a lot more.

How much did the world mean to God? What did he think it was worth? I used to have a poster that said: 'I asked Jesus how much he loved me. "This much," he said, and he stretched out his arms and died.'

We may not know why we're suffering, but at the cross we learn something of God's character. Jesus thought the world was worth dying for. He willingly chose a horribly painful death to pay the price for our brokenness and to show us how much he loves us. God thinks you and I are worth it.

Ruth

BIG QUESTIONS: HOW CAN GOD ALLOW SUFFERING? PART 4

Jesus' life and death show us that he loves us, shares our pain and thinks we are worth rescuing. But Jesus rising from the dead helps us make sense of the cross and provides a way out of our suffering.

When Jesus said, 'It is finished' on the cross, he didn't just mean his life. He meant that our sins and the power they hold over us have been removed (Romans 6.7). He also meant that death itself has been defeated (1 Corinthians 15.54). If Jesus rose again, death is not the end (for 'proof' of the resurrection, see 16 March).

When Aslan comes back to life in C. S. Lewis's *The Lion, the Witch and the Wardrobe*, he says that: 'when a willing victim who had committed no treachery was killed in a traitor's stead, the Table would crack and Death itself would start working backwards'.

Tragically, we still experience death, but when we lose someone we're reminded to grieve as those with hope (1 Thessalonians 4.13) because we know this isn't the end of the story. If this world isn't as God created it to be, it certainly isn't how he intends to leave it. One day, he will return and put an end to our suffering. Revelation 21.4 says: 'He will wipe every tear from their eyes, and there will be no more death or sorrow or crying or pain. All these things are gone forever' (*New Living Translation*)

Our God is so compassionate and gentle that his own hand will wipe away our tears.

We have a future hope where there will be no more pain. Or, as J. R. R. Tolkien puts it in *The Return of the King*, where everything sad will come untrue.

When life is so painful it's a struggle to even breathe, I don't always want to know *why* I'm suffering. I want someone to pull me out of my situation and hold me in the pain. Jesus' life, death and resurrection may not tell us why we're suffering, but they do show us we're not alone, and it's not for ever.

Ruth

16 DEC

You are not the mistakes
you have made.

17 DEC

Bit by bit, person by person, Jesus is drawing people to
himself.
He is longing for his creation to be united with him.
His hope is for the disconnected to become connected,
the hopeless to become hopeful,
and for the lost to be found.

18 DEC

Jesus said:

Your Father knows what you need before you ask him.
This, then, is how you should pray:

'Our Father in heaven,
hallowed be your name,
your kingdom come,
your will be done,
on earth as it is in heaven.
Give us today our daily bread.
And forgive us our debts,
as we also have forgiven our debtors.
And lead us not into temptation,
but deliver us from the evil one.'
Matthew 6.8–13

A FIRM FOUNDATION

I overheard a girl in a coffee shop say, 'They've let me down. I just don't trust anyone any more.' I sat there feeling so sad at hearing her say that. Have you ever felt like that? That your trust has been broken and you feel hurt?

Today I want you to know an amazing truth – God can be trusted. There's a story in the Bible about a man building his house on the sand . . .

> Therefore everyone who hears these words of mine and puts them into practice is like a wise man who built his house on the rock. The rain came down, the streams rose, and the winds blew and beat against that house; yet it did not fall, because it had its foundation on the rock. But everyone who hears these words of mine and does not put them into practice is like a foolish man who built his house on sand. The rain came down, the streams rose, and the winds blew and beat against that house, and it fell with a great crash.
> Matthew 7.24–27

God's words can be trusted. He is someone so stable and so secure that you can build your life on him with absolute certainty that he will never let you down.

What are you building your life on? People let us down, they make mistakes and break our trust, but God will *always* be reliable. He is a firm trustworthy foundation, and when we build our life on his words we can be completely sure that it will withstand any storm.

20 DEC

Comparison is the thief of joy.

Theodore Roosevelt,
26th President of the USA

21 DEC

HOW DOES THE MEDIA AFFECT US?

I recently conducted some research to work out how and why teenage girls are using Instagram. The results were really insightful, but one statistic in particular stood out to me. I discovered that 78 per cent of teenage girls mainly use Instagram 'to see what other people are doing'. As well as this being what other people choose to post online, it also encompasses what other people comment on and 'like' or don't 'like' online.

When it comes to social media, it becomes very clear that our focus seems to be on other people (but in a negative way). We get totally engrossed in their lives, their opinions, their posts, their likes.

This can be really detrimental when we allow social media (and the comments and 'likes' of others) to define our self-worth. We need to let go of those things. We need to move away from comparison towards inspiration, where we can be encouraged by what we see without it negatively affecting our own sense of self.

When we let go of things, we need to take hold of new things — new ways of thinking and being. I came across the following verse in the Bible: 'God pays no attention to what others say (or what you think) about you. He makes up his own mind' (Romans 2.11, *The Message*).

How freeing is that? To know what God's mind says about who we are requires time spent in his presence, listening to him and reading his word.

The reality of who we are is who God created us to be. Spend time with him today and invite him to tell you who he's made you to be.

Jessie

22 DEC

Guide me on the road
to eternal life.

Psalm 139.24, *The Message*

MISCONCEPTIONS

I was once babysitting a little girl called Ella, who was four years old. It was just before Christmas and we spent the evening singing Christmassy songs (I loved it!). Before Ella went to bed, I said to her, 'Ella, what does Father Christmas ride on?'

'A tractor,' she replied.

I laughed, a lot, and said, 'A tractor? No, what flies through the sky? What do the reindeers pull?'

'A tractor!' she insisted, and then very innocently added, 'Farmer Christmas rides on a tractor!'

I fell about laughing. *Farmer* Christmas, haha! It was such a cute moment.

For four years of her life, Ella had believed that the man who comes down the chimney and brings her presents was a farmer. I decided to let her mum set her straight in case she got upset that the farmer wasn't going to come this year.

Just as Ella had misconceptions about Father Christmas, we can often believe misconceptions about God. Often, we think that we need to earn God's love by being good. But that's not right. Father Christmas's gift-giving might be dependent on our behaviour, but God's isn't at all. God delights to give good things to his children, not on the basis of what we do but on the basis that we are his children (Matthew 7.11). At Christmas, God gave us a Saviour, Jesus, not because we deserved it but because he loved us (1 John 4.10).

Let's give God thanks this Christmas for the gift of his Son, Jesus, who came down to save us from our sin and bring us back to the Father.

24 DEC

For to us a child is born,
    to us a son is given,
        and the government will be on his shoulders.
And he will be called
    Wonderful Counsellor, Mighty God,
    Everlasting Father, Prince of Peace.

Isaiah 9.6

25 DEC

GOD PROOF

I clearly remember sitting on my bed at the age of seven and staring at a cardboard box on the top of my wardrobe. We were moving house and we had boxes everywhere. I should have been going to sleep but I sat there in the dark and said quietly, 'God, if you're real, move that box off the wardrobe.'

I waited and waited, and it didn't move. I was disappointed and went off to sleep questioning God's existence at the grand old age of seven. (Can you imagine how freaked out I'd have been if a cardboard box had flown across my room?)

Years later, at the age of 26, I sat in my local pub with a friend who had previously been a Christian and he said, 'If you can get Jesus to walk into this pub, then I'll believe.'

The way he spoke reminded me of the cardboard box incident.

'I want proof' – that's what many people say. Only God doesn't need to prove himself to us. He invites us to search for him, to seek him, to speak to him, to desire him and put our trust (however shaky that may be) in him, to develop a faith in him.

I *love* the verse in Jeremiah where God says, 'I will be found by you' (Jeremiah 29.14).

The question is, are you looking for him?

You don't have to wait for the End. I am, right now, Resurrection and Life. The one who believes in me, even though he or she dies, will live. And everyone who lives believing in me does not ultimately die at all. Do you believe this?

John 11.25–26, *The Message*

27 DEC

COVERED IN LOVE

Some of the most powerful and encouraging words in the whole Bible are these: 'See what great love the Father has lavished on us, that we should be called children of God! And that is what we are!' (1 John 3.1).

The word 'lavish' means to heap, cover, smother and shower. The love God has for us is not given begrudgingly and it is not rationed. It is *lavished*. Too often we treat God's love like a really limited data allowance; we can only have a little bit at a time for fear it will run out when we need it most. But we're meant to live in love unlimited. His love for us is all-you-can-eat, not a starvation diet. We are meant to live in the life-giving love of our Father God.

Take a moment to think about how much you are loved by God. How does that make you feel? Do you find it easy to accept and enjoy? Do you find yourself believing that you're loved reluctantly or do you know you're loved relentlessly? Ask God to help you live more and more knowing how completely and wonderfully loved you are.

Ali

28 DEC

MOVING THE MOUNTAIN

There's a popular kids' song, which is often sung in Sunday schools. The lyrics are 'Faith as small as a mustard seed will move mountains.'

It might sound like a strange way of talking about faith, but it's been done deliberately. If you immediately cast your imagination to what a mountain looks like, you'll picture a huge, steep rock face. If you then try to picture a mustard seed, you'll be picturing almost the total opposite, right? Mustard seeds are actually only one or two millimetres in diameter! And so what is the Bible trying to say here?

Just as the song says, Matthew 17.20 tells us that we only need to have faith as small as a mustard seed in order to do amazing things for God's kingdom. In Jesus' day, he would sometimes heal people and tell them that their faith had made them well. This doesn't mean that God only heals people if our faith reaches a certain level; instead, it means that even a small amount of faith in God can make truly extraordinary things happen.

At the same time as emphasizing the fact that we only need mustard seed faith to move mountains, there's the fact that this faith can *move mountains* if we put it into action. We can sometimes *think* we have some level of faith, only to find ourselves doubting, stressing and worrying as soon as any trial comes our way. So what this verse (and lyric) actually means is that we need to take faith seriously. Just *saying* we have it is only half of the story. Truly believing that God can and will come through in our lives is the most powerful position to stand from and it's what it looks like to have mountain-moving faith.

Walk in *faith* today and trust that God is more than able.

Naomi

29 DEC

God won't leave you, he won't lie to you, he won't turn his back on you, he won't give you more than you can handle, he won't abuse you, he won't push you around, he won't pressure you, he won't force you, he won't manipulate you, he won't drop you, he won't abandon you, he won't cheat you, he won't break you, he won't hate you, he won't ignore you.

Instead, God will love you, he will challenge you, he will comfort you, he will defend you, he will refresh you, he will discipline you, he will forgive you, he will hold you, he will see you, he will understand you, he will save you, he will listen to you, he will change you, he will heal you, he will support you, he will catch you, he will teach you, he will lead you.

30 DEC

HOPE

I use the word 'hope' a lot; do you?

I hope you have a nice day!
I hope I do well in the test.
I hope I'm not getting a cold.

Hope is a state of expectation, a want, a desire. Hope is always within us, like water in our bodies, but sometimes we experience pain and trouble in our lives, much like a drought. We think our hope is dried up and gone; we are thirsty and feel weak. But that hope is still there, and from that small drop of water, hope can burst out with power, like a waterfall.

How can hope rise in our life and quench our thirst? How can we see floods of joy and expectation fill our lives? By putting our hope in the One who never fails.

Hope is *trusting* in our Father God, who will never fail us.
Hope is *receiving* his love that will always surround us.
Hope is *knowing* that he will for ever be our help.

Because of his love our hearts can be full of expectation, hope and excitement for life.

I love the way it's put by theologian John Piper: 'Biblical hope is not just a desire for something good in the future, but rather, biblical hope is a confident expectation and desire for something good in the future' (desiringGod.org).

Without this biblical hope, life is just wishful thinking. What hope is there to be found without God? Hope and faith go hand in hand. When we're despairing, our hope in God picks us up. Hope is always in us, and it can always rise up. My question to you is — what, or whom, are you putting your hope in?

31 DEC

REFERENCES

Note: The sources of quotations in *Hope Rising 365* found only on social media or internet quotation sites (such as Instagram, Twitter or <www.brainyquote.com>) are not listed.

Ailis Brennan, 'Every person who appears in the The Black Eyed Peas star-studded 2016 remake of "Where is the Love?"', *GQ* (2 September 2016).
Arthur Conan Doyle, *The Sign of the Four* (1890).
Richard Dawkins, *River out of Eden: A Darwinian view of life* (London: Weidenfeld and Nicolson, 1995).
Lisa Firestone, 'The benefits of generosity', <www.huffingtonpost.com/lisa-firestone/the-benefits-of-generosit_b_5448218.html?guccounter=1>, last accessed 20 December 2018.
Richard Foster with Kathryn A. Helmers, *Celebration of Discipline: The path to spiritual growth* (London: Hodder & Stoughton, 2008).
Rachel Gardner, *Beloved* (Nottingham: IVP, 2015).
Rachel Gardner, *Cherished: Boys, bodies and becoming a girl of gold* (Nottingham: IVP, 2009).
Victor Hugo, *Les Misérables* (1862).
John Lennox, *Gunning for God* (Oxford: Lion, 2011).
C. S. Lewis, *The Great Divorce* (London: Touchstone, 1996).
C. S. Lewis, *The Lion, the Witch and the Wardrobe* (London: HarperCollins, 2009).
C. S. Lewis, *The Magician's Nephew* (London: HarperCollins, 2009).
C. S. Lewis, *Mere Christianity* (London: HarperCollins, 2016).
John O'Donohue, *To Bless the Space Between Us: A book of blessings* (London: Doubleday, 2007).
Michael Ots, *What Kind of God?* (Nottingham: IVP, 2008).
John Piper, <www.desiringgod.org/messages/what-is-hope>, last accessed 20 December 2018.
Peter Sutcliffe, 'May the peace', from 'Morning Office', in Northumbria Community, *Celtic Daily Prayer* (London: HarperCollins, 2005).
J. R. R. Tolkien, *The Return of the King* (London: HarperCollins, 2011).

COPYRIGHT ACKNOWLEDGEMENTS

COPYRIGHT ACKNOWLEDGEMENTS (continued)

Scripture quotations from the *Holy Bible, New Living Translation* are copyright © 1996, 2004, 2007. Used by permission of Tyndale House Publishers, Inc., Carol Stream, Illinois 60188, USA. All rights reserved.

The publisher and authors acknowledge with thanks permission to reproduce extracts from the following:

29th Chapter, 'Saviour'. Quoted by kind permission of 29th Chapter.
Hannah Atkins, 'If Life Were Some Music', from *Falling*. Quoted by kind permission of Hannah Atkins.
Paul Booth, 'Who Put the Colours in the Rainbow?'. © Paul Booth (Adm. by Song Solutions www.songsolutions.org). All rights reserved. Used by permission.
Kathryn Scott, 'Hungry'. © 1999 Vineyard Songs UK (Adm. by Song Solutions www.songsolutions.org). All rights reserved. Used by permission.

First published in Great Britain in 2019

Society for Promoting Christian Knowledge
36 Causton Street
London SW1P 4ST
www.spck.org.uk

Copyright © Meg Cannon 2019

British Library Cataloguing-in-Publication Data
A catalogue record for this book is available from the British Library

ISBN 978–0–281–07857–8
eBook ISBN 978–0–281–07858–5

1 3 5 7 9 10 8 6 4 2

Designed and typeset by The Woodbine Workshop
Printed in Great Britain by TJ International

eBook by Manila Typesetting Company

Produced on paper from sustainable forests